TAUNTON'S

**FOR PROS BY PROS**®

BUILDER-TESTED | CODE APPROVED

# Cabinets, Vanities & Countertops

FROM THE EDITORS OF

**FineHomebuilding**

The Taunton Press

**The Taunton Press**
Inspiration for hands-on living®

The Taunton Press, Inc., 63 South Main Street, PO Box 5506, Newtown, CT 06470-5506
e-mail: tp@taunton.com

Editor: Christina Glennon
Copy Editor: Seth Reichgott
Indexer: Jay Kreider
Cover design: Alexander Isley, Inc.
Interior design: Carol Singer
Layout: carol singer | notice design
Cover photographers: (Front cover): Rob Yagid, (Back cover): Nat Rea

*Fine Homebuilding*® is a trademark of The Taunton Press, Inc., registered in the U.S. Patent and Trademark Office.

The following names/manufacturers appearing in *Cabinets, Vanities, and Countertops* are trademarks: 3M®, Accuride®, Armstrong®, Avonite®, Bertch®, Benjamin Moore®, Blum®, Bondo®, Bosch®, Canyon Creek®, Ceramithane®, ClingCover®, Corian®, Craft-Art®, DeWalt®, DeWils®, Dekton®, Diamond®, Durock®, EcoTop®, Enkeboll®, EnviroGLAS®, Festool®, Floor-Shell®, Formica®, Freud®, General®, Graco®, Grass®, Hafele®, IceStone®, IKEA®, Jesada®, Klip Biotechnologies®, Knape & Vogt®, KraftMaid®, Lie-Nielsen®, Makita®, Marshalltown®, MasterBrand Cabinets®, Merillat®, Minwax®, Plain & Fancy Custom Cabinetry®, Paperstone®, Pionite®, Rev-A-Shelf®, Richlite®, Scotch®, SharpShooter®, Sherwin-Williams®, Shetkastone®, Silestone®, Smooth-On®, Styrofoam®, Swanstone®, Titebond II®, Trewax®, Ultraglas®, Vetrazzo®, VytaFlex®, Waterlox®, Wellborn Cabinet, Inc.®, West System®, White River®, Wilsonart®, Windex®, Woodcraft®

LIBRARY OF CONGRESS CATALOGING-IN-PUBLICATION DATA
CABINETS, VANITIES & COUNTERTOPS / AUTHOR, EDITORS OF FINE HOMEBUILDING.
  PAGES CM
 INCLUDES INDEX.
 ISBN 978-1-63186-161-1
1. CABINETS, VANITIES AND COUNTERTOPS 2. CABINETWORK. 3. COUNTERTOPS. I. FINE HOMEBUILDING.
TT197.C236 2015
684.1'6--DC23
        2015010213

PRINTED IN THE UNITED STATES OF AMERICA
10 9 8 7 6 5 4 3

ABOUT YOUR SAFETY: Homebuilding is inherently dangerous. From accidents with power tools to falls from ladders, scaffolds, and roofs, builders risk serious injury and even death. We try to promote safe work habits through our articles. But what is safe for one person under certain circumstances may not be safe for you under different circumstances. So don't try anything you learn about here (or elsewhere) unless you're certain that it is safe for you. Please be careful.

## ACKNOWLEDGMENTS

Special thanks to the authors, editors, art directors,
copy editors, and other staff members of *Fine Homebuilding* who
contributed to the development of the articles in this book.

# Contents

Cabinets are equally important to the architectural style and practical functionality of a home. From the perspective of the former, cabinetry has as much potential, if not more, than any other element of a home to define its style. Whether traditional, modern, or somewhere in between, proportions, construction details, hardware, and color must all be carefully considered. And they must all work together. Not one of these aspects takes precedent. If you're planning to buy your cabinets, you'll be in good hands with many manufacturers of stock, semi-custom, and custom cabinets who have poured decades of design resources into getting the look of many architectural styles right. It may still be up to you, though, to wisely choose complimentary hardware and color and to choose materials and construction methods that will yield durable storage in your kitchen or bath.

When it comes to function, it's important to carefully consider how you live. If you grocery shop in bulk at big box stores, you may need a pantry cabinet in your kitchen. Open shelves are trendy in kitchens and baths right now, but are you neat enough to keep your dishware and towels on display? The simple decision between doors and drawers in a vanity or the lower cabinets in a kitchen is actually quite personal and requires you to examine what you will store in each and how often you will need to access it. Choosing doors just to save money may be a decision that ends up costing you more in frustration than it was worth.

If you are looking for ways to save some money that won't come back to haunt you, you've found the right book. Building and/or installing your own cabinets is not only a way to save money, but it also is rewarding work. And it's work that anyone armed with the right tools and some professional advice can tackle. That's what *Fine Homebuilding* is all about: Professional builders sharing their hard-learned lessons with anyone who wants to do their own work, and do it right. Covering everything from choosing, building, and installing cabinets to making your own countertops with laminates, wood, and concrete, you find everything you need for great kitchen cabinets, bathroom vanities, countertops, and more on these pages. I hope you find this book and your project inspiring, useful, and, most importantly, fun.

Build well,
Brian Pontolilo
Editorial Director, *Fine Homebuilding*

# Refinish Your Cabinets

BY PHILIP HANSELL

Refinishing kitchen cabinets is a difficult and labor-intensive painting project, but the payoff can be huge. For a fraction of the cost of new cabinets, refinishing can transform a well-worn kitchen into one that looks and feels new.

As with most painting projects, the secret to a high-quality finish on kitchen cabinets is proper preparation and the right tools and materials for the job. Here, I describe how my painting company goes about refinishing cabinets in a typical kitchen. The project shown is a high-end kitchen remodel in a handsome brick house in one of the nicest neighborhoods of Durham, North Carolina.

The kitchen design called for new tilework, lighting, and appliances. Although the built-in appliances required new cabinets, the existing cabinets were in good shape, so the homeowners decided to save thousands of dollars by refinishing their existing kitchen cabinets.

## Spraying Works Best

Unless the client's budget is supertight, we generally paint kitchen cabinets with an airless sprayer. Spraying costs more than brushing because of the additional masking and setup, but a high-quality sprayer in the hands of an experienced painter produces a flawless, glass-smooth finish that's as good as or better than the factory finish on most mass-produced cabinets.

My company paints so many cabinets every year that we installed a spray booth in our shop. It's the same type of enclosure you'd find in an auto-body shop. Before we bought the booth, we made spray enclosures by hanging drop cloths or tarps from our shop ceiling. Tarp enclosures work fine, particularly if you'll be doing this only once, but the booth—with its bright lights and filtered air—provides a better finish in less time.

You can spray cabinets on site, too. In fact, we almost always spray cabinet boxes on the job because it's too time-consuming and expensive to remove them. Unfortunately, on most job sites it's tough to find a space large and clean enough to spray the many doors and drawers found in a typical high-end kitchen, which is why we do those in our shop.

## Getting Started

The first step is protecting the countertops and floor with heavy kraft paper. If the kitchen has hardwood flooring that won't be refinished at the end of the project, we put down a thicker product called FloorShell® (www.trimaco.com). We tape the paper or FloorShell around the perimeter and at seams to prevent the high-pressure sprayer from lifting it during spraying. We also cover appliances, light fixtures, backsplashes, and adjacent walls with ClingCover® plastic drop cloths (www.trimaco.com) taped in place.

Refrigerators need fresh air for operation, so we leave the plastic sheeting off the intake grilles until we're ready to spray. When it's time to spray, we turn off the refrigerator and cover the grille until we're done for the day. We always tell the homeowners about this ahead of time so that they can consume or move anything that's particularly perishable.

## Remove Drawers and Doors

Once the space is protected, we remove the cabinet drawers and doors. Because cabinet doors have hinges adjusted for the individual cabinet box, we

**LABEL EVERYTHING.** To make reinstalling the doors and drawers easier with a minimum of hinge adjustments, the crew carefully labels and bundles the hinges and marks their locations. A piece of tape covers each mark so that it won't be painted over. The marks are located so that they'll be hidden when the kitchen is put back together. Cabinet doors are marked behind a cup hinge. The mark indicates which cabinet box the door came from.

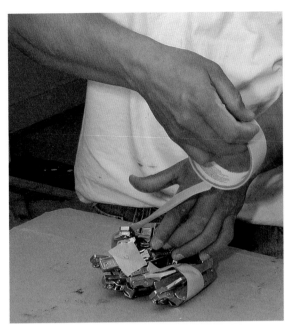

BOXES. Cabinet boxes are marked behind a hinge mount. The void in the finish will be hidden by the hinge.

HINGES. Individually labeled hinges are grouped by cabinet door and taped together. Bundles are labeled, too.

carefully label the doors, hinges, and cabinets so that everything can be returned to its original location when the job is done. This saves us from having to readjust the hinges. We do the labeling in an inconspicuous spot and cover the identifying marks with tape so that they won't be obscured with paint when the part or cabinet is sprayed.

We remove pulls and knobs before stacking the doors and drawers in our trucks. With the drawers and doors removed, we mask the drawer slides and accessory hardware, but we don't mask shelf standards because they look better when they're painted to match the cabinet color.

## Surface Prep

After everything in the kitchen is masked, we fix any dents or scratches and sand the cabinet boxes with 320-grit paper. Afterward, we dust off the boxes with an old paintbrush and a shop vacuum equipped with a bristle-type nozzle. After vacuuming, we wipe everything down with a damp rag and then a tack cloth.

DRAWERS. Pullout shelves and drawers are labeled on the back side of the back panel to keep the marks hidden.

SAND AND CLEAN. Once the floor is covered with kraft paper and adjacent surfaces and hardware are masked, any damage is filled with auto-body filler, sanded with 150-grit paper, and then spot-primed with sprayed oil primer. Finally, all previously painted surfaces are sanded with 320-grit paper. Using 320-grit paper at the end creates a smooth surface for priming and painting. Changing sandpaper frequently yields quicker results.

Previously stained cabinets are fully sanded with 150-grit paper and then wiped down with lacquer thinner before we spray on an oil-based primer.

## Oil Works Best

We use oil products on most of our kitchen-cabinet jobs. Oil-based paint bonds and covers better than water-based products, and it sands more easily. In addition, oil paint and primer dry more slowly than latex, so any overspray has a chance to blend in with the coating that has been sprayed on top of it. Waiting too long to cover the overspray, though, will make the surface appear rough. To minimize the rough surface caused by overspray, we spray upper cabinets first and then the lower cabinets below, and we consistently work from one end of a cabinet run to the other.

## The Right Gear

For finishing the cabinets, we use a Graco® 395 or 695 sprayer with a 310 fine-finish tip, which has a 6-in. spray pattern. Thinning the paint or primer is not required unless the product is especially cold, which makes the solvents more viscous. It's better to let the paint or primer warm to room temperature, however, because thinned coatings don't cover surfaces as well.

We spray primer on the inside of the cabinet box first, and then we prime the exterior. When the cabinet backs are exposed, such as on an island or a peninsula, we spray all the individual cabinet backs at the same time. Once the cabinets are fully primed and dry, we sand everything again with 320-grit paper before spraying on the topcoat.

CLEAN UP. Once everything is sanded, the kitchen is given a thorough cleaning, first with a shop vacuum and then with a damp rag. Just before spraying, cabinet surfaces are wiped with a tack cloth. All masking materials must be secured fully to prevent them from lifting during spraying.

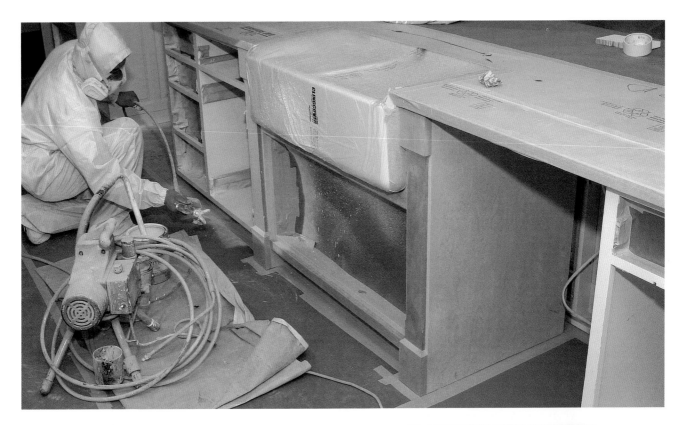

**PRIME AND PAINT.** Both old and new cabinet boxes are coated first with an oil-based primer. The author and his crew start with a bank of upper cabinets, then spray the lower cabinets below. They work in the same direction for both upper and lower cabinets. Painting and priming in this order ensures that any overspray is covered with wet finish before the overspray dries. Dried overspray leaves a rough surface.

**SPRAY IN SEQUENCE.** Insides are sprayed first, starting with the top, then the sides, bottom, and back. On the cabinet exterior, the crew starts with the sides and then sprays the front. When cabinet backs are exposed (on islands and peninsulas), all backs are sprayed at the same time by working from one end to the other, like a typewriter.

## The Right Paint

Our favorite paint for cabinets is ProClassic oil-based paint from Sherwin-Williams®. We apply it in the same order as the primer. The secret to spraying is to apply the paint in multiple thin layers to prevent drips and sags, which have to be sanded out.

It's also important that the paint be fully atomized for even coverage. If you see that the spray pattern is formed by dots larger than $\frac{1}{32}$ in., or if there are discernible lines at the top and bottom of the spray pattern (called fingering), the paint is too thick, or you need more pressure.

Don't use a spray tip that is overly worn, and don't spray at too high a pressure. Both of these situations result in excess overspray, which wastes paint and results in a smaller spray pattern prone to drips. It's also important to hold the spray nozzle parallel to the cabinet and to start moving before pulling the trigger.

When we're done spraying, we check our work with a bright light. We make any needed touch-ups and then let the paint dry for at least 48 hours.

## Reassembly

Leaving the floor and countertop protection in place, we remove the masking inside the cabinet boxes and reinstall the doors and drawers. Then we remove the rest of the masking by working from the top down so that any falling paint flakes won't stick to the freshly painted surface.

**TAKE DOORS TO THE SPRAY BOOTH.** Few residential construction sites have a space large and clean enough to prep and spray dozens of drawers and cabinet doors. The author takes these items to his spacious shop, where they can be prepped and then sprayed in his automotive-style spray booth. To start, gouges are filled with body filler, sanded with 150-grit paper, and spot-primed. The whole surface is sanded with 320-grit paper before painting and priming.

**FRONT, BACK, BACK, FRONT.** Fronts are sprayed first, followed by two coats on the back. Finally, a second coat goes on the front, minimizing handling damage to the most visible side.

The final step is to reinstall the pulls. We also install new bumpers on the drawers and doors at this time. I like clear plastic bumpers, which are durable and soften the impact of a slamming cabinet door. Because fresh latex paint sticks to plastic bumpers, we use felt bumpers with latex paint.

**FINISHING TOUCHES.** The last part of the job is to reinstall the door and drawer pulls. When the job calls for new hardware, the author fills the old holes, but it's the general contractor's job to drill new holes and install the new hardware. New drawer and door bumpers also are installed at this time: plastic bumpers for oil paint, felt bumpers for latex paint.

# A Buyer's Guide to Kitchen Cabinets

BY SCOTT GIBSON

Cabinet manufacturers from all over the country roll out their best stuff for the kitchen and bath industry's annual springtime trade show. When I last attended, kitchen cabinets of every style were sprinkled among booths showcasing bathtubs and appliances. Every style from Arts and Crafts in quartersawn oak to modern in Macassar ebony was available. Wellborn Cabinet Inc.® alone offered nearly 1,500 different combinations of finish and door styles.

Yet for all this diversity, every cabinet is made from the same basic components. Where they differ, and why prices vary so widely, can be traced to what's under the hood: materials, hardware, and construction techniques. Although manufacturers offer such a wide price range that they can cater to budgets of any size, spending more money usually means greater durability, better hardware, a nicer fit and finish, and more flexible designs.

A competitive scramble among stock and semicustom cabinet manufacturers gives buyers more choices than ever. Stock cabinets, the most economical, are still essentially an off-the-shelf commodity with the fewest options in finish and materials. Semicustom cabinets allow buyers to specify most but not all features. Prices vary accordingly.

While cabinet sizes in both categories tend to be standardized (available for the most part in 3-in. increments), manufacturers have tried to make it easier for buyers to order the options they want even on a modest budget.

Custom cabinets can be whatever a buyer is willing to pay for, usually with the longest lead time and the highest prices. In the end, how a cabinet is made is a lot more important than what it's called. The essential elements to consider are box construction, drawers, doors, hardware, and finish.

DOVETAILED DRAWERS

SOFT-CLOSE HINGES

FULL-EXTENSION DRAWER SLIDES

# DESIGN WITH YOU IN MIND

THE SAME KITCHEN DESIGN doesn't work for every homeowner, so a new generation of designers have sharpened their pencils to match their products with the lifestyles of potential buyers. Whether you're a first-time homeowner or a retiree, someone has been thinking about you.

In fact, Heather Argo, a designer for the cabinet manufacturer KraftMaid®, invented "Edward" to help design a kitchen for Gen-Y buyers. A 20-something lawyer in Philadelphia, Edward likes games and electronics, doesn't cook much, and needs lots of storage for bottled water and ready-to-eat food. The result? A modern kitchen with a clean, white finish, contemporary hardware, a big TV cabinet, and a raised circular counter for eating or playing cards.

KraftMaid's layout for "active seniors" includes a built-in desk with an adjacent full-height pullout for office and cleaning supplies (see the photo at right). Armstrong®, another manufacturer, has taken a similar "lifestyle solutions" approach. Among its offerings are a cabinet doubling as a children's play area (see the photo below) and a chef's zone that keeps cooking tools and other accessories within a couple of feet of the cooktop.

To Wellborn Cabinet's Kimberly Dunn, it's a question of providing "more customization on every level." Buyers are less likely to follow broad trends these days than they are to buy cabinets that suit their needs and tastes exactly. "Everybody wants what they want," she says, "not just what their neighbor just bought."

**KITCHEN OFFICE.** A desktop flanked by a full-height rollout by KraftMaid provides storage for office supplies and space for paying bills.

**PLAYTIME.** With toys and a writing surface close at hand, Armstrong's play center can be a part of kitchen activity, but not underfoot.

## Go for Plywood Boxes, Even if You'll Never See Them

A box, or carcase, is the foundation of any kitchen cabinet. Hidden behind face frames and end panels, the box is often unseen, but everything depends on its structural integrity.

Where you'll find significant differences is in the materials that go into the sides and back of the box. Economy cabinets usually are made of particleboard covered with a thin layer of vinyl printed with a wood-grain pattern. Particleboard is inexpensive, which helps keep the cost of the cabinets down, but it doesn't hold screws as well as plywood, and it is susceptible to water damage. If the vinyl surface tears or becomes delaminated, there's no way to repair it.

Melamine is a type of pressed wood-fiber panel that's often used for cabinet boxes because the plastic layer on top is easy to keep clean. It's heartier than the vinyl-covered particleboard in economy cabinets, but the surface can chip if it's abused.

Plywood costs more, but it's inherently more robust. Screws that attach hinges, drawer slides, and other hardware are less likely to be pulled out over time, and the surface can be repainted or refinished if it's damaged.

Cabinet sides range in thickness from $\frac{1}{2}$ in. to $\frac{3}{4}$ in. Thin walls can make a cabinet feel cheap, and they offer less meat for shelf pins and hardware screws to grab. Plywood a full $\frac{3}{4}$ in. thick makes a solid, long-lasting box that can support heavy counters without complaint.

Cabinet backs aren't that important. Even good-quality cabinets might have backs made of $\frac{1}{4}$-in. material. There is a structural purpose—the back prevents the cabinet from racking—but unless the countertop is unusually heavy or drawer hardware is to be mounted directly to the back, a panel that's $\frac{1}{4}$ in. thick shouldn't be a drawback. Still, plywood is a better choice than hardboard.

Face frames also help make the box sturdy. They are usually made from the same hardwood as the drawer faces and doors. Look for gap-free joints between the pieces that make up the frame. When inside edges around door and drawer openings are sanded smooth and joints are tight, it's an indication the frame was made with care. In frameless cabinets (also known as European cabinets), doors and drawers hide the front of the box completely. Without a frame to help keep the box rigid, it's more important than ever to buy a cabinet made of high-quality $\frac{3}{4}$-in. material.

## Dovetails Are Stronger, so the Drawers Last Longer

Hardwood drawer sides that are $\frac{5}{8}$ in. or $\frac{3}{4}$ in. thick are a good idea on all but the lightest and smallest drawers. Material that's only $\frac{1}{2}$ in. thick, especially if it's particleboard, is not as dependable.

Drawer bottoms are often $\frac{1}{4}$ in. thick, and again, plywood is a better choice than particleboard or hardboard. On cabinet pullouts that carry a lot of weight, a $\frac{3}{8}$-in. or even a $\frac{1}{2}$-in. plywood bottom is less likely to sag over time.

Well-made dovetail joints make the most-durable drawers. A poorly made dovetail, on the other hand, is no better than a poorly made anything else. There should be no gaps in the interlocking parts, and the joint should be sanded and finished carefully. Particleboard drawers are typically glued and stapled at the corners and don't stand up well to heavy use.

Wood drawers are by far the most common, but metal-sided drawer boxes like Blum®'s Tandembox

### GOING GREEN

A SIGNIFICANT NUMBER OF CABINET manufacturers have won "green" certification from the Kitchen Cabinet Manufacturers Association's environmental stewardship program. If you're interested in sustainable options for your kitchen, go to www.kcma.org.

# YOU GET WHAT YOU PAY FOR

## IKEA READY-TO-ASSEMBLE

- **Box:** ¾-in. frame-less melamine
- **Drawers:** Metal sides, melamine front and bottom
- **Doors:** Melamine
- **Hardware:** Adjustable cup hinges, integral drawer slide
- **Finish:** Plastic
- **Price:** $

## WELLBORN STOCK

- **Box:** ½-in. particleboard sides, ¾-in. hardwood face frame
- **Drawers:** Stapled ¾-in. particleboard
- **Doors:** Hardwood frame and panel
- **Hardware:** Euro cup hinges, epoxy-coated drawer slides
- **Finish:** Stain with clear coat
- **Price:** $$

**PARTS THAT FIT.** Thanks to careful machining, the precut and predrilled cabinet parts go together easily. Assembly of the 24-in. base unit took about 90 minutes.

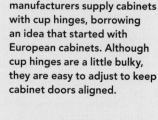

**EURO HINGES RULE.** Many manufacturers supply cabinets with cup hinges, borrowing an idea that started with European cabinets. Although cup hinges are a little bulky, they are easy to adjust to keep cabinet doors aligned.

**INTEGRAL SLIDES. IKEA** supplies snap-together drawers that combine adjustable metal sides with integral drawer slides. A melamine drawer front matches the rest of the cabinet.

**BASIC DRAWERS.** Particleboard drawers that have been stapled together are a potential weak spot. These epoxy-coated drawer slides are three-quarter extension and make access to the back of the drawer difficult.

---

or IKEA®'s ready-to-assemble cabinets have a sleeker, more contemporary look. They're well adapted to frameless cabinets, and some come with integrated full-extension drawer slides and a soft-close feature. They can be paired with a variety of dividers and organizers.

## Solid Wood Doesn't Always Make the Best Door

Cabinet doors come in two basic types: frame and panel or slab. Frame-and-panel doors are the traditional choice with face-frame cabinets and are avail-able in dozens of styles. The frames are typically made of solid wood, while the panels might be solid wood or veneered medium-density fiberboard (MDF).

Veneered panels are flat and stable, and furniture history proves there is nothing structurally inferior about them. However, they might age differently than a solid-wood frame, resulting in a contrast between the two. This is an issue only with woods that change dramatically with age, such as cherry, but the concern is worth considering. Solid-wood panels are more likely to shrink and expand with

### ARMSTRONG SEMICUSTOM

- **Box:** ½-in. plywood, ¾-in. hardwood face frame
- **Drawers:** Stapled ½-in. hardwood sides, plywood bottom
- **Doors:** Hardwood frame and panel
- **Hardware:** Adjustable cup hinges, epoxy-coated slides
- **Finish:** Stain with catalyzed clear top coat
- **Price:** $$$

### PLAIN & FANCY CUSTOM CABINETRY®

- **Box:** ½-in. plywood, ¾-in. face frame
- **Drawers:** Dovetailed ⅝-in. hardwood
- **Doors:** Frame and panel
- **Hardware:** Pin hinges, full-extension undermount drawer slides
- **Finish:** Antiqued paint
- **Price:** $$$$

**PLYWOOD UPGRADE.** Plywood is stronger and more durable than particleboard. It's usually available as an upgrade.

**STURDY CABINET BOX.** Plywood components and wood glue blocks, rather than stapled plastic corner braces, are signs of a well-made, fully custom cabinet.

**ROLLOUTS FOR CONVENIENCE.** The cup hinges are standard, but the two rollouts on the inside of this cabinet offer more convenient storage than shelves.

**OUT OF SIGHT.** These undermount drawer slides allow the drawer box to roll all the way out. They're hidden beneath the drawer, so all you see are the drawer sides and the carefully machined dovetails.

changes in humidity, but won't show color differences and won't delaminate. Solid-wood panels are probably worth their slightly higher cost.

Slab doors are either glued-up solid wood or veneered MDF and are typically used with frameless cabinets. A substrate of MDF should help keep the door flat and free of warp. A solid-wood door that's 18 in. or 20 in. wide might cup or twist over time.

No matter what the style, look at the doors carefully. On frame-and-panel doors, the joints should be tight and free of gaps when the cabinets are new.

If the panels are glued up from solid wood, look for a good match in grain and color between adjacent boards. No cross-grain sanding marks should be visible on either the inside or the outside of the door, and the finish should feel soft and silky.

If the door has a glass panel, the fit between glass and wood should be neat, and you should not find globs of glue or caulk oozing out of the seam.

## Hardware Should Stand up to Wear and Tear

Hardware manufacturers have pulled out all the stops to make cabinet interiors more functional and user-friendly. Most cabinet companies buy hardware from the same manufacturers, so no matter what brand of cabinet you buy, you should have a good menu of hardware to choose from.

Most drawers and pullouts ride on side-mounted ball-bearing metal slides. A variety of types are available as full extension or three-quarter extension, meaning the drawer either comes all the way out or stops with about a quarter of its depth still buried inside the cabinet. Full-extension slides are well worth the extra cost.

Slides are rated by the weight they are designed to carry, typically 75 lb. or 100 lb. Slides rated at 75 lb. should be fine for all but the largest and heaviest drawers, but roll-out pantry shelves or drawers for heavy pots and pans or appliances do better with beefier slides.

Undermount slides are becoming increasingly common. They are attached to the bottom of the

drawer and are hidden by the drawer sides, making the cabinets look more like furniture.

Many cabinet companies now equip their drawers with a soft-close mechanism made by Blum called "Blumotion." It grabs the drawer near the end of its travel, slows it down, and then gently brings it to a stop—a great idea if you live in a house where people tend to slam drawers closed.

Good luck finding cabinets with traditional butt hinges. European-style door hinges, or cup hinges,

**PANTRY IN A DRAWER.** A wire organizer in an Armstrong base cabinet makes it possible to stow a great deal of supplies in a small space without losing track of anything.

**FOLD-OUT STORAGE.** This storage unit in an Armstrong base cabinet eliminates wasted space in the corner. Racks fold open and roll out from the cabinet on ball-bearing slides.

**RECYCLING CENTER.** DeWils® Custom Cabinetry offers a revolving recycling center in this corner base cabinet, making good use of an often awkward space. The rack holds three plastic bins.

**UP AND AWAY.** These upper cabinet doors from Wellborn pop up to provide full access without conventional hinges.

**ROUNDABOUT.** A wire lazy Susan in this DeWils cabinet provides plenty of storage and better visibility than an organizer with solid shelves.

**FLEXIBLE STORAGE.** A full-height rollout from Kraft-Maid provides storage for office supplies on one side and cleaning supplies on the other, making the most of a narrow cabinet. (See the other side in the right photo on p. 14.)

## SOURCES

**ARMSTRONG**
www.armstrong.com

**BLUM**
www.blum.com

**DEWILS**
www.dewils.com

**IKEA**
www.ikea.com

**KRAFTMAID**
www.kraftmaid.com

**PLAIN & FANCY CUSTOM CABINETRY**
www.plainfancycabinetry.com

**WELLBORN CABINET INC.**
www.wellborn.com

have taken over. They are available for both frameless and face-frame cabinets, and because they allow a variety of adjustments, these hinges make it easy to hang even finicky inset doors. The Blumotion soft-close feature is also available for hinges.

## Fancy Finishes Are Durable, Too

Manufacturers devote a lot of energy to cabinet finishes, what might be the most fickle part of the business as designers try to gauge shifting buyer preferences. The tremendous diversity of painted, glazed, stained, and distressed finishes is a testament to the industry's effort to appeal to any taste.

In general, the least-expensive finishes are simple clear coats. The most expensive are multilayered glazes and paints, crackle finishes, and rub-through painted surfaces that take more time to execute at the factory. Painted surfaces are somewhat less durable than clear finishes and might show slight gaps in joinery more readily. Glazed-paint finishes can help disguise these minor flaws.

For clear finishes, most manufacturers use a conversion varnish, a tough two-part catalyzed coating. Old-schoolers might prefer lacquer because it's more repairable, but catalyzed finishes are extremely durable and are now the norm.

Where you're likely to find differences is in the quality of application. The best finishes start with thorough surface prep, meaning you should see no sanding marks of any kind on the finished surface. Whether the surface is matte or glossy, it should be smooth and blemish free. Look along edges and inside doors, using your fingers as well as your eyes.

In the end, finishes are largely a matter of personal taste. Basic, no-frills finishes should provide a long service life, but if you want something more elaborate and are willing to pay for it, you have plenty of options.

# Souped-Up Stock Cabinets

BY GARY STRIEGLER

I've been a builder for more than 25 years, and one of my favorite expressions is, "The older I get, the better I was." It's natural to think that things in the past were always better, and quite often it's true. However, one big exception is the cabinets and millwork available to builders these days.

With modern technology, cabinet shops can turn out boxes in almost any size or configuration. But even if you're limited to standard cabinets from a home center, they can be arranged in such a way to add visual interest to any kitchen. The trick is to stop thinking about cabinets in what's come to be known as the streamlined approach. We've all seen kitchens composed of 24-in.-deep, 36-in.-tall base cabinets and equally uniform upper cabinets starting at 18 in. above the counters and ending at the ceiling. These regimented rows of boxes offer plenty of storage, but they also can be just plain boring.

To turn cabinets into eye-catching arrangements that add beauty to an ordinary kitchen, I use a strategy called coastlining. I arrange cabinets next to one another so that their lines move in and out, and up and down, like the variations in a rocky shoreline. These differences in height and depth offer several powerful opportunities for visual juice. Shadows formed where cabinets of different depths intersect are prominent places to add detail. And outside corners created by upper cabinets of varying depths create lots of places to play crown moldings to great effect.

I have a talented crew that does wonderful finish work. So it makes sense, both economically and efficiently, to get basic cabinets from a shop and put my crew to work dressing them up with moldings and carvings. Even the biggest kitchens can be transformed with just a few hundred feet of custom molding.

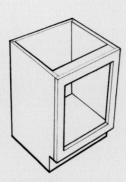

## BEYOND THE BASICS

Standard boxes plus stock moldings can transform any kitchen from dull and dreary to dazzling and delightful.

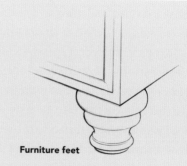

**Furniture feet**

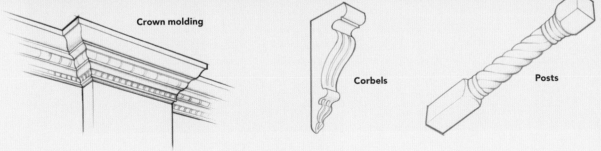

**Crown molding**

**Corbels**

**Posts**

This is where the fun and creativity live: in the details. We use drawer fronts, end panels, rope moldings, toe-kick treatments, turned legs, pilasters, corbels, furniture feet, and plenty of crown molding to customize each kitchen we build. (The moldings in this article are from White River®; see suppliers on p. 25.) The variations are practically limitless, from white beaded cabinets in a farmhouse kitchen (see the photo on the facing page) to the walnut-stained look of a baronial armoire (see p. 21). The boxes are similar, but the finishes and details differ.

Kitchen islands are another opportunity to make something special out of ordinary boxes. I call this strategy massing, which is the arrangement of cabinet boxes to create places for appliances, shelves, or sitting areas. Organized this way, the spaces between the cabinets can be equally useful.

## Coastlining Cabinets

Varying the height and depth of the cabinets creates broken lines that are the foundation for an exciting kitchen (see the photo at right). Wall cabinets can be kept even with the ceiling, where continuous crown molding will conceal the cabinet-ceiling joint. Installing some cabinets lower than others also can make the kitchen look as if it was added on to over time. Cabinets for appliances such as a wall oven or range hood are perfect opportunities to add different depths to the wall arrangement.

Appliances such as stovetops also create the possibility of varying the depth of base cabinets. The height of base cabinets can vary, too, for specific work areas such as a bread-making station.

Using different cabinet-base treatments for cabinets of varying depths lends the look of assembled furniture to a kitchen. In the photo at right, the oven cabinet at the far end has a solid base. The recessed cabinet next to it has a deep toe kick to allow for furniture feet. The stovetop cabinet sports a traditional toe kick, whereas the end cabinet also has its toe kick recessed for furniture feet.

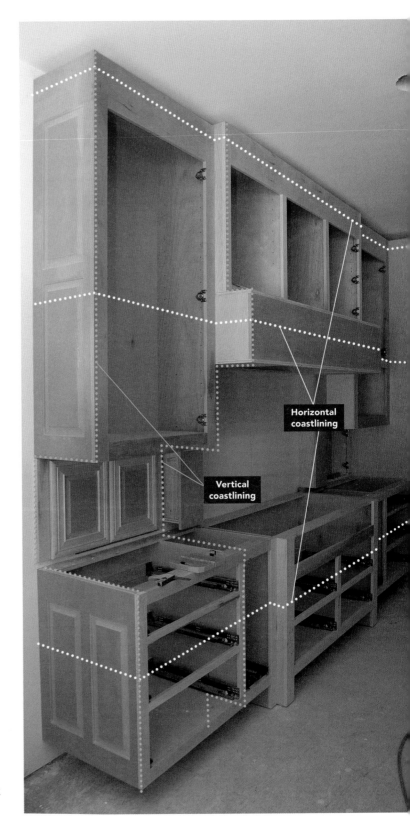

Horizontal coastlining

Vertical coastlining

# ISLAND MASSING

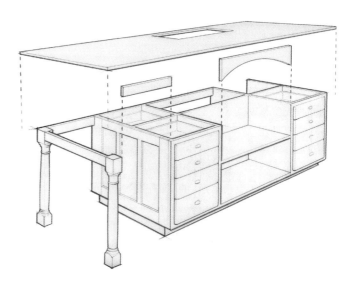

### SOLID MASSING
Keeping the cabinet boxes tight to one another and then applying corner posts, end panels, and a solid base can give an island the feel of a massive piece of furniture to anchor the kitchen.

### OPEN MASSING
Moving the corner posts away from the cabinets to create a sitting area produces negative space, which lets the island float in the kitchen. A traditional toe kick further augments the effect. Keeping the cabinet boxes apart and finishing the spaces between them as display cases or bookshelves reduces the massive feel of a big island.

**ADD INTEREST.** To prevent a boring island, include variety in the form of doors, appliance stations, drawers, and seating areas.

## Massing Islands

Kitchen islands too often look like a chunk of utilitarian space added to the middle of a kitchen, clunky and uninviting. Breaking up the cabinet-base treatments and varying the cabinets from doors to drawers to appliance stations can add immediate interest to an island grouping (see the photo above).

## Styling on Site

Once the cabinet configuration is established, decorative elements boost the effects of coastlining and cabinet groupings. Every time a molding turns a corner, that corner becomes more apparent. And as we've seen, this effect works for both stain-grade as well as paint-grade cabinets. For base cabinets, ornamental corner posts augment the coastlining effect. Whereas crown molding and edgebanding provide an overall effect in the kitchen, additional moldings can enhance specific areas. Decorative corbels add visual support to wall cabinets at openings, such as over a sink or a stove. Frames of smaller band molding can make raised end panels come alive. Applied pilasters visually minimize the frames around cabinet doors and drawers, and carvings can add an accent to a bare expanse, such as the housing for a range hood.

### DECORATIVE MOLDING SUPPLIERS

**A. LEWIS MANUFACTURING CO.**
800-969-2212
www.alewismfg.com

**ADAMS WOOD PRODUCTS**
423-587-2942
www.adamswoodproducts.com

**ARCHITECTURAL INNOVATIONS**
336-889-2001
www.architecturalinnov.com

**ARCHITECTURAL MOULDING AND MILLWORKS**
888-942-6626
www.mouldings.cc

**CUMBERLAND WOODCRAFT CO.**
www.cumberlandwoodcraft.com

**ENKEBOLL® DESIGNS**
800-745-5507
www.enkebolldesigns.com

**OSBORNE WOOD PRODUCTS INC.**
800-849-8876
www.osbornewood.com

**OUTWATER PLASTICS INDUSTRIES INC.**
800-631-8375
www.outwater.com

**ROYAL BUILDING PRODUCTS**
800-368-3117
www.royalmouldings.com

**SIERRA STAIR WORKS INC.**
916-652-2800
www.sierrastairworks.com

**VINTAGE WOODWORKS**
903-356-2158
www.vintagewoodworks.com

**WHITE RIVER**
800-558-0119
www.whiteriver.com

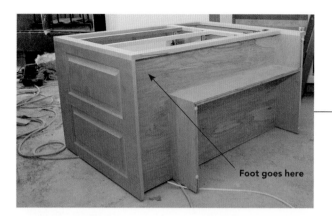

Foot goes here

Crown molding

Framed
raised panel

Edgebanding

**FURNITURE FEET.** Furniture feet give the cabinets the look of, well, furniture. The toe kick on the cabinets is held back from the front to make it less visible (above). Blocks keep the furniture feet above the finished-floor height (top). They screw to the cabinets from inside.

**TO CUT THE FEET TO THE RIGHT HEIGHT,** screw them to a simple jig that makes cutting them with a miter saw fast and safe. And remember that for kitchen cabinets the feet might look better upside down.

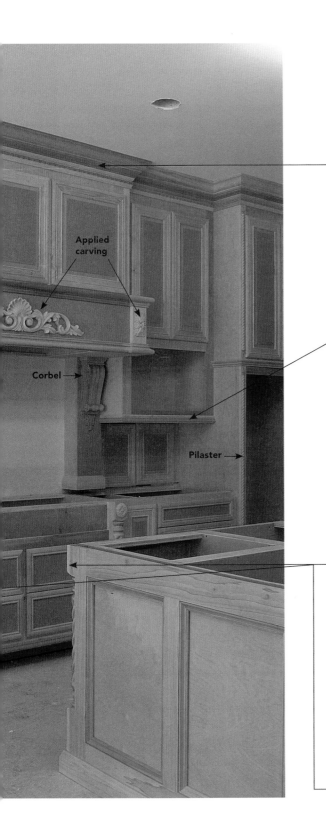

Applied carving

Corbel →

Pilaster →

**MOLDINGS.** Crown wraps the top edge of the cabinetry to finish the intersection between wall cabinets and ceiling. A layer of panel molding adds to the decorative effect.

**STANDARD PANEL MOLDING** acts as an edgebanding along the bottom edges of both wall and base cabinets to give the cabinets weight and to balance the visual effect of the crown above.

**DECORATIVE POSTS.** Manufactured ornamental posts can enhance a coastline corner in the base cabinetry. Two cuts on a tablesaw (bottom) create an outside corner post that wraps the cabinet corner (left). Don't throw out the "waste" pieces. They can be used to finish an end panel, such as on the island in the photo at far left.

# Get to Know Semicustom Cabinets

BY NENA DONOVAN LEVINE

I
f your kitchen cabinets are decades old and you're homing in on a renovation, consider this advice: "Ya gotta know the territory." It's from *The Music Man*, a show as old as those very cabinets. Dispensed by a traveling salesman headed for River City, it's also a great mantra to use when surveying today's kitchen-cabinetry landscape.

In 2012, the cost of an average kitchen renovation was over $47,000, according to a National Kitchen and Bath Association member survey. Cabinetry consumes one-third or more of that amount. You can do the math, but it is safe to say this investment deserves careful consideration.

There are three broad categories of kitchen cabinets: Stock cabinets tend to be the most affordable but offer the least variety of style and finishes, are sometimes made from lower-quality materials, and may be constructed for a shorter useful life. Custom cabinets are at the other extreme in that they can be made of familiar or exotic materials to any size, style, and quality. Semicustom cabinets fall between stock and custom cabinets and are arguably the best value. The Kitchen Cabinet Manufacturers Association defines semicustom as "built to order but within a defined set of construction parameters; available in standard widths but with more choices for depth and height modifications." According to one of the organization's recent member surveys, the semicustom category makes up 46 percent of the overall market.

MasterBrand Cabinets® has lines in all three categories. Stephanie Pierce, manager of MasterBrand's design studio, says that unlike the company's stock line—which is limited to very specific dimensions, styles, and finishes—its semicustom lines, including Diamond and Decorá, offer designers and builders "flexibility within limitations." More specifically, these brands' offerings can be customized only to the degree of the shops' capabilities. At the custom end of the spectrum, MasterBrand's Omega Cabinets will outsource any fabrication that its shop is not capable of.

## Snapshot of a Giant Category

Semicustom cabinets are built upon receipt of an order, so lead time is longer than it would be for stock cabinets, which you can sometimes get off the shelf at a home center. It's shorter than it would be for custom cabinets, however, although this varies based on the complexity of the cabinets and the builder's availability. Merillat's® semicustom Classic line can ship in as little as five to ten days. Canyon

Creek's® Katana line has a lead time as short as four weeks from order to delivery. Certain upgrades can push lead times out to six weeks or more.

Semicustom cabinets are offered in standard 3-in.-wide increments from 9 in. to 45 in. For an upcharge, you can modify this to ⅛ in. Such precise dimensions reduce the call for filler strips and minimize wasted space. Standard cabinet depths and heights also can be increased or decreased for an upcharge. So if using a standard 24-in.-deep base cabinet doesn't allow adequate clearance in a pantry or a passageway, you can reduce the box depth and still use the particular cabinets you were hoping for. Standard wall cabinets are 30 in. and 36 in. tall, but sometimes 33 in. or even 42 in. works better with a

particular ceiling height. Again, with most semi-custom lines this level of customization is possible.

Semicustom cabinets are available with face-frame or frameless construction or both. The choice is mostly aesthetic: Face frames are more common on traditional-style cabinets, and frameless cabinets are more contemporary looking. But there are plenty of exceptions.

On face-frame cabinets, the doors can be inset or they can be overlaid to reveal more or less of the

frames. The hinges attach to the face frames. Doors on frameless cabinets cover the cabinet box's finished front edge. Door hinges attach to the box sides. Frameless construction offers a more open interior and is typical of today's European cabinetry. In the United States, by contrast, face-frame construction outsells frameless, according to Danielle Mikesell, Merillat's director of marketing. Both traditional and frameless cabinets can be ordered with a panoply of door and drawer styles, wood species, finishes, crown-molding profiles, and box-construction options. Some manufacturers will even combine

face-frame construction with a frameless aesthetic. When it comes to style and construction, most of what is commonly built by custom-cabinet shops can be found in semicustom cabinets.

Cabinet doors and shelves are typically ¾ in. thick. A loaded ¾-in. shelf can span a 36-in.-wide cabinet, whereas thinner shelves may bow across that span. Full-depth shelves, adjustable in ½-in. increments, maximize storage. For organizing cabinet interiors, there are plenty of accessories, such as roll-out shelves and lazy Susans. Companies such as Häfele®, Knape & Vogt®, and Rev-A-Shelf® make

**NO WASTED SPACE.** This clever end-panel door from MasterBrand makes the most of a few unused inches for magazine storage and office supplies.

**HARDWARE MATTERS.** Most manufacturers offer hardware options to enhance storage in their cabinets. Some can be outfitted with aftermarket hardware as well. These Diamond® cabinets have elegant and useful storage that keeps cookware from getting lost deep inside the island.

bins, baskets, and recycling containers to complement semicustom lines.

Semicustom lines offer warranties that may equal the limited-lifetime warranty typical for custom cabinets. Canyon Creek, Merillat, and KraftMaid all offer such warranties on some lines that cover the product for as long as the purchaser owns it, with certain exclusions. Unfinished products are excluded, for example, as are normal wear and tear, instances of abuse, and improper installation. Merillat's Classic, also a semicustom line, has a 25-year warranty.

# WHAT'S NOT SEMICUSTOM

**THE DISTINCTION BETWEEN STOCK,** semi-custom, and custom cabinets can be blurry. Some manufacturers, like Merillat, offer lines in more than one category. Here's a look at the alternatives to semicustom.

## STOCK

"Stock" refers to cabinet inventory stocked—and sometimes stacked—at a manufacturer or retailer. Options for door style, wood species, finish, molding profile, and hardware are limited to what's there. Materials reflect a budget price point; for example, a stock cabinet door may be ½ in. thick, whereas a semicustom or custom door measures ¾ in. Cabinet-box size is limited to 3-in.-wide increments from 9 in. to 45 in. Depths for both wall and base cabinets are fixed, and warranties are the shortest on the market—often five years or less. Benefits of stock cabinetry include its entry-level price and fast (immediate or within a few days) delivery. Stock quality may suit a rental unit, starter house, or budget kitchen. Limited choices may inspire DIY creativity and yield excellent value.

## CUSTOM

"Custom" cabinets, originating in a small shop or a large manufacturing facility, are built to client specifications upon receipt of the order. They can incorporate curved doors, complex angles, odd box sizes, and unusual colors. If you want to hand-select or book-match exotic veneers, you can. Options for door style, wood species, finish, crown-molding profile, box selection, accessories, and hardware are enormous. Benefits of custom cabinetry include vast choice, tailored fit and finish, and individualized fabrication. Expect a premium price tag and longer remodel time, because custom lead times run eight weeks to several months. Large manufacturers offer generous (even lifetime) warranties for custom products. Small-shop warranties vary. Custom implies top quality, but it's not a given from every small cabinet shop.

## Four Ways to Assess Quality

Experts agree on what distinguishes a quality semi-custom cabinet: box construction, drawers, doors, and finish. In addition, hardware—drawer slides and door hinges—should be well-made and adjustable. Blum, Grass®, and Häfele are examples of top-quality hardware brands.

### BOXES

Today's semicustom cabinet boxes can be made from plywood, particleboard, or medium-density fiberboard (MDF). Even if different boxes meet the same testing requirements and have equal warranties, there are variations to note in the materials used.

To begin with, not all plywood is created equal. There are different grades, and the number of plies can vary. Assuming high-quality glue and fabrication methods are used, the more plies a panel has, the more stable the panel will be. Plywood is typically the most expensive option for cabinet boxes.

Another option, formaldehyde-free particleboard (sometimes called furniture board) is not the cheap, porous particleboard of the past. It is a dense and durable substrate for veneer and is often more affordable than plywood cabinet boxes. It can be sized and cut with great precision, as can MDF.

MDF is made from recycled wood fibers and resin. As the smoothest of the three box materials, it is an excellent substrate for both veneer and paint. MDF's downside is its heaviness.

## Drawers

You're likely to find dovetailed and doweled drawer construction in most semicustom cabinet lines. Both are equally sturdy, though dovetails add character and a high-quality appearance. You won't likely find glued or stapled drawers in semicustom cabinets. If you do, consider upgrading. Dovetails and dowels not only look better, but they last longer.

For a durable drawer, the hardwood or MDF fronts should be applied to a four-sided drawer box, not used as the fourth box side. Drawer boxes typically have ½-in.- or ¾-in.-thick solid-wood sides,

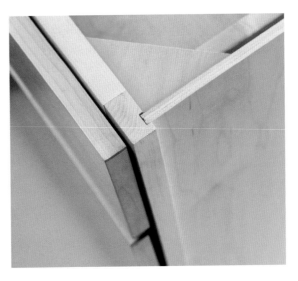

**BOXES.** Cabinets are most often made of plywood, particleboard, or MDF.

**DRAWERS.** Look for dovetailed or doweled drawers, which are sturdier than drawers that are glued or stapled.

although Canyon Creek's semicustom lines feature a ½-in.-thick plywood drawer box. A drawer bottom of ³⁄₁₆-in.-thick plywood resists deflection even when fully loaded. Some semicustom European lines offer metal drawer boxes; a different look, it's perhaps the most durable option available.

When it comes to drawer hardware, full-extension slides separate semicustom cabinets from most stock offerings and provide full access to the contents of a drawer. Undermount slides support the drawer from the bottom; their concealment is aesthetically preferable to side-mounted slides, particularly with dovetailed drawers. A soft-close feature, available on many semicustom cabinets, means they'll close quietly and without slam damage. Avoid drawers that shake or rattle when you operate them, which is a sign of cheap drawer slides.

## Doors

Doors don't express a cabinet's overall quality as reliably as the other three items. Even lesser-quality cabinets may have reasonably well-built doors. In any event, look for $3/4$-in.-thick doors made of hardwood, painted or veneered MDF, or veneered particleboard. Good particleboard is dense (Merillat Classic doors call for 48-lb. particleboard). All doors should have rubber bumpers to cushion their closing action and adjustable hinges from a reputable manufacturer.

**DOORS.** Doors aren't as clear an indicator of quality as boxes or drawers, but they should be high quality with good hardware.

Most doors consist of a four-piece frame plus a center panel. A center panel needs room to move in response to humidity, but that doesn't mean it should rattle around in the frame. A center panel may be hardwood or veneer, but its grain and color should closely match the frame. High-quality doors have a raised center panel set into the door frame facing either outward (a raised-panel door) or inward (a recessed flat-panel door). Raised panels—whether facing in or out—possess a thickness and solidity that distinguishes them from a $1/4$-in.-thick flat center panel. Because they do not respond to changes in humidity, MDF doors in a raised-panel style are made of a single piece of material.

Door-edge, frame, and raised-panel profiles can be varied to individualize a semicustom door style, though not every style will be available for both framed and frameless cabinets. There are also laminate and thermofoil door options, but they are more commonly found in stock cabinetry.

## Finish

Finish choices vary as much as door styles. Canyon Creek, for example, offers nearly 40 standard stain and paint colors on more than 10 wood species. Glazing, distressing, burnishing, and antiquing add subtle finish variations. Canyon Creek will also mix a finish color to match a paint-store chip.

Stain finishes comprise several steps, usually including stain application, heat curing, one or more sealer coats, and a topcoat. Cabinets are sanded by machine and by hand prior to staining, then sanded again between sealer coats. Companies typically cure stains, sealers, and topcoats with convection heat. The resulting baked-on finish is durable enough to support extended warranties. Bertch® Cabinetry uses a blend of alkyd, amino, and vinyl resins in its sealers; the topcoats are alkyd and amino resins formulated into catalyzed conversion varnish. Sheen levels can be modulated from matte to glossy by varying the topcoat formulation, but all sheens should be equally durable.

FINISH. Between stains and paints and finishing options such as glazing, distressing, burnishing, and antiquing, your choices are nearly endless. Look for a finish that is clear, not cloudy, and drip free.

## SOURCES

There are far too many semicustom cabinet manufacturers to list. Here are a few to get you pointed in the right direction. To dig deeper, go to a local kitchen showroom or visit the Kitchen Cabinet Manufacturers Association website (www.kcma.org).

**CANYON CREEK CABINET COMPANY**
www.canyoncreek.com

**KRAFTMAID CABINETRY**
www.kraftmaid.com

**MASTERBRAND CABINETS, INC.**
www.masterbrand.com

**MERILLAT**
www.merillat.com

"Painted" finishes are achieved using colored (opaque) catalyzed conversion varnishes. These dry harder than standard paint. Even when a semicustom manufacturer matches, say, a Benjamin Moore® color, the resulting paint differs from what's available in retail because the cabinetry formulation must be sprayable and yield more sheen. The paint typically is applied as a primer coat topped with one or more additional coats, with sanding and heat-curing in between. Not all painted finishes receive a separately formulated topcoat as stain finishes do.

A painted finish must be applied to a smooth surface, so paint-grade maple is often used. Because this finish sits on the wood surface instead of moving into the wood like a stain, a painted finish can crack when the wood under it moves. Hairline cracks appear at door and face-frame joints, and are not considered defects. However, the finish should not peel or flake. Most manufacturers offer matching paint for touch-ups along with a cabinet order.

To assess a finish, you need to see actual product samples. The finish should be clear; a cloudy appearance is a sign of poor quality. It should be smooth and drip-free, without visible sanding marks. Molding and door edges should be crisp, with no finish buildup. Low- or no-VOC formulations are desirable.

WHY SO MANY LINES? MasterBrand Cabinets alone has nine cabinet lines ranging from stock to custom. Its semicustom lines include Homecrest, Schrock, Kemper, Kitchen Craft, Diamond, and Decorá. According to Stephanie Pierce, MasterBrand's design studio manager, each brand is tailored to a slightly different customer.

FOR FUNCTION. MasterBrand's Diamond line, shown here and above, is designed and marketed toward busy homeowners who value flexibility and function.

## We Can't Tell You What It Will Cost

It would be great to read an article or visit a website and get a firm figure for what your cabinets might cost, but it's not that simple. Calculators, such as at www.FineHomebuilding.com/cabinet-calculator, can give you a range, but the offerings of semicustom cabinetmakers are vast, and even some seemingly logical questions—such as whether face-frame or frameless cabinetry is more expensive—are not so easy to answer.

Let's explore that example: Frameless boxes ought to be ¾ in. thick to provide good purchase for door hardware, whereas a face-frame box can be ⅝ in., because door hardware is not attached to the box. So frameless cabinets, in general, must be more expensive. But without face frames, those European-styled cabinets don't use as much hardwood or require as much labor. So it seems that traditional cabinets must be more expensive. But filler strips can mar the clean lines of modern, frameless cabinets, so you'll want to specify custom box dimensions, increas-

FOR STYLE. MasterBrand's Decorá line, shown above and below, is meant for style-savvy homeowners who want lots of options for personalizing their kitchens.

ing the cost. You still haven't specified a door and drawer style, a finish, or all the storage upgrades you want.

In short, distinguishing by frameless or traditional construction, dovetail or dowel joinery, or one particular feature or finish is not a meaningful way to compare prices. For every instance where one company's product costs more, there are others where you will find the opposite. Showrooms offering semicustom lines have a list of "retail" prices for every component in a cabinetry manufacturer's line. (Merillat's 2011 book for its Masterpiece line runs 664 pages.) What the showroom charges a customer, however, depends first on its discount calculation—a percentage assigned by the manufacturer—and then on how it adjusts that discount to cover its cost of business. The discount calculation varies based on the dollar volume of that cabinetry line sold by that showroom, among other factors.

The purchaser's price for a kitchen with dozens of components might include upcharges for customized dimensions, premium wood species, certain finishes and hardware, or glass doors (which require

a finished cabinet interior). How badly a showroom wants the business can also affect price comparisons between showrooms. With so many factors influencing the final price, you'll have to talk to a designer or dealer to get a legitimate estimate.

# Build Better Cabinets with the Best Plywood

BY MATTHEW TEAGUE

Choosing the right plywood for your next cabinetry project entails more than just picking the species you want and backing your truck up to the loading dock. With plywood prices ranging from $35 for a 4×8 sheet to well into the $100s, you want to make sure you're spending money where it counts: on structurally sound cores where it matters and on fine veneers where they're visible.

## Core Options

Plywood is commonly available in four different core combinations. Each has unique features that can affect the strength and look of cabinets, whether they are stain grade or paint grade.

### VENEER CORE

This plywood has multiple layers of thin (usually $1/7$ in. and thinner) solid wood that's glued up in a cross-grain orientation. Typical $3/4$-in. plywood is made of five $1/7$-in. core layers and two face veneers. Although this is the strongest of all core options, imperfections in the core veneers can telegraph through to the face veneers, leaving surfaces that are not perfectly smooth. That said, superior strength, screw retention, and light weight make it appealing to work with.

### MDF CORE

This plywood has a solid piece of MDF in place of the five core layers in veneer-core plywood. Weight and dust are two downsides, but MDF creates a dead-flat panel that doesn't have any telegraphing issues. Screw retention is good, though it's best to drill pilot holes and to use fasteners designed for engineered wood, like Confirmat screws. The edges of MDF-core plywood can be profiled and finished, unlike other plywood that must be edgebanded in most applications.

### PARTICLEBOARD CORE

Particleboard-core plywood is similar to MDF-core plywood in both construction and characteristics. The panels are flat, retain fasteners well (with the same caveats as MDF), and are among the least expensive plywood sheets available. However, particleboard-core plywood is the most susceptible to tearout when cutting, routing, or drilling.

### COMBINATION CORE

Combination-core plywood consists of a traditional veneer core, except that the outer layers of the core are made of MDF. Combi-core, as it's often called, offers (almost) the best of both worlds: the smooth, flat faces characteristic of MDF and the strength attributes of veneer core. It's also only slightly heavier than veneer core.

### SO WHICH CORE OPTION IS BEST FOR ME?

There's little dispute that an MDF core produces the smoothest, flattest surface, making it the best choice where finishing is concerned. Keep in mind that painted plywood is subject to the same considerations as clear-finished or stained plywood. Paint can actually be worse at highlighting irregularities in the plywood face. If you're looking for an easier material to work with, choose combi-core plywood, which offers nearly the same performance attributes.

**VENEER CORE** offers superior strength, at a price.

**MDF CORE** is the best choice for a smooth finish.

**PARTICLEBOARD CORE** is cheap, but difficult to work.

**COMBINATION CORE** has a strong core and a smooth face.

## THE BEST PLYWOOD FOR EACH PART

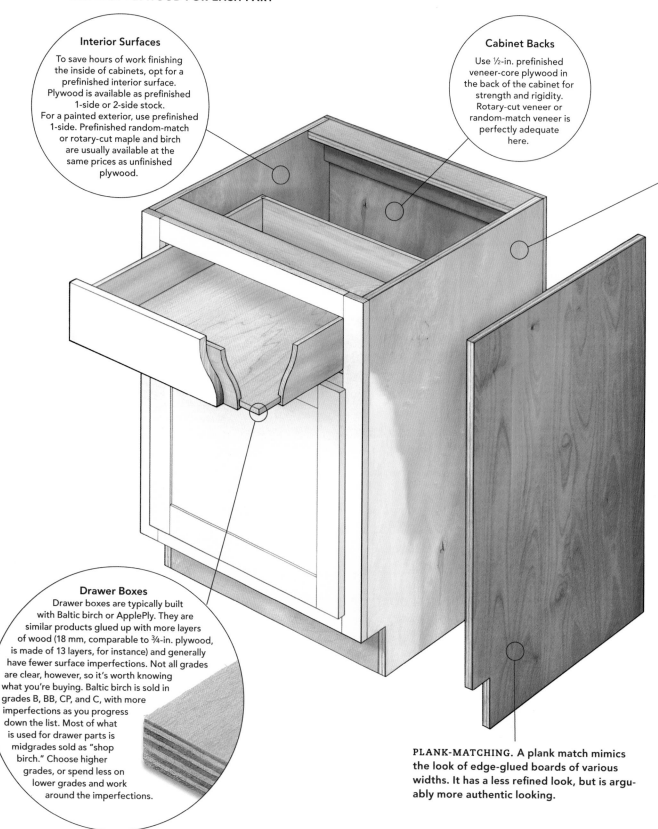

**Interior Surfaces**
To save hours of work finishing the inside of cabinets, opt for a prefinished interior surface. Plywood is available as prefinished 1-side or 2-side stock. For a painted exterior, use prefinished 1-side. Prefinished random-match or rotary-cut maple and birch are usually available at the same prices as unfinished plywood.

**Cabinet Backs**
Use ½-in. prefinished veneer-core plywood in the back of the cabinet for strength and rigidity. Rotary-cut veneer or random-match veneer is perfectly adequate here.

**Drawer Boxes**
Drawer boxes are typically built with Baltic birch or ApplePly. They are similar products glued up with more layers of wood (18 mm, comparable to ¾-in. plywood, is made of 13 layers, for instance) and generally have fewer surface imperfections. Not all grades are clear, however, so it's worth knowing what you're buying. Baltic birch is sold in grades B, BB, CP, and C, with more imperfections as you progress down the list. Most of what is used for drawer parts is midgrades sold as "shop birch." Choose higher grades, or spend less on lower grades and work around the imperfections.

**PLANK-MATCHING.** A plank match mimics the look of edge-glued boards of various widths. It has a less refined look, but is arguably more authentic looking.

ROTARY-CUT VENEER, as shown here, is suitable for painted surfaces and hidden parts. Sliced veneer is best for stained or clear-finished components.

BOOKMATCHING. This A-grade cherry veneer is bookmatched, so the grain patterns mirror each other across the panel. It's among the most attractive orientations, particularly for stain-grade cabinets.

## Veneer Options

Plywood veneers are either rotary-cut or sliced. Rotary-cut veneers are produced from the log in the same way you pull tape from a roll. The cut produces a wild, variegated grain pattern that is cost-effective but generally less attractive. Sliced veneer is cut from the log in much the same way a log is cut into lumber, so it yields veneer that mimics solid stock rather well.

### ROTARY-CUT VENEER

Rotary-cut veneer is a perfectly adequate and economical veneer for use on hidden parts of a cabinet, like the back and the drawers. For the exterior and interior faces of painted work, a rotary-cut veneer with a B or better grade is sufficient. Opt for either birch or maple. (See the sidebar at right for an explanation of veneer grading.)

### SLICED VENEER

Of all the ways that sliced veneers can be oriented, you'll most commonly find bookmatched and random-matched orientations. Bookmatching looks the best in most applications. It has alternating sheets of veneer from a single flitch opened like a book to create a mirrored-grain pattern. Common on back faces, random-match veneers cost the least, but vary in width, color, and grain. Plank-matched veneer is a good option on exposed faces. It's usually a special order and is laid up in a deliberately mismatched pattern to look more natural.

### WHICH VENEER OPTION IS BEST FOR ME?

For cabinets receiving a clear or stained finish, use a B or better face veneer. For the back veneer, select a 1 or 2 grade, depending on the project. Bookmatched faces look best when the splice is centered on a panel, even if it results in added waste. If a panel is so wide that it includes a second splice line, the mirrored effect becomes lost or muddled. In these cases, a plank match would be a good option. For the inside of the cabinet, a rotary-cut or random-match veneer is perfectly suitable.

### VENEER GRADING

VENEERS FROM A LOG are segregated according to appearance into six face grades (AA, A, B, C, D, E) and four back grades (1, 2, 3, 4), with back grades being aesthetically inferior. The best face and back veneers are clear, whereas successive grades have more noticeable characteristics, such as knots, mineral streaks, and color variation.

Plank-matched cherry, face-grade A

Plank-matched cherry, face-grade B

Plank-matched cherry, face-grade C

# 6 Rules for Fast and Foolproof Cabinetmaking

BY SVEN HANSON

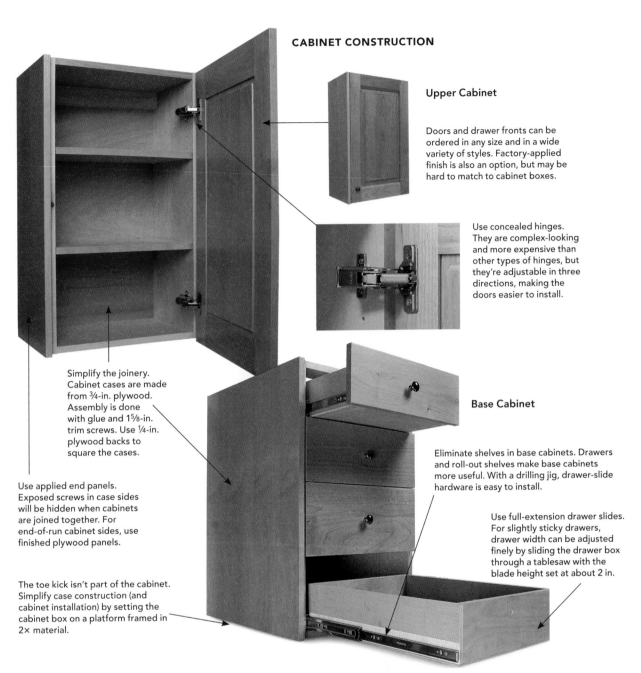

**Upper Cabinet**

Doors and drawer fronts can be ordered in any size and in a wide variety of styles. Factory-applied finish is also an option, but may be hard to match to cabinet boxes.

Use concealed hinges. They are complex-looking and more expensive than other types of hinges, but they're adjustable in three directions, making the doors easier to install.

**Base Cabinet**

Eliminate shelves in base cabinets. Drawers and roll-out shelves make base cabinets more useful. With a drilling jig, drawer-slide hardware is easy to install.

Use full-extension drawer slides. For slightly sticky drawers, drawer width can be adjusted finely by sliding the drawer box through a tablesaw with the blade height set at about 2 in.

Simplify the joinery. Cabinet cases are made from ¾-in. plywood. Assembly is done with glue and 1⅝-in. trim screws. Use ¼-in. plywood backs to square the cases.

Use applied end panels. Exposed screws in case sides will be hidden when cabinets are joined together. For end-of-run cabinet sides, use finished plywood panels.

The toe kick isn't part of the cabinet. Simplify case construction (and cabinet installation) by setting the cabinet box on a platform framed in 2× material.

I n my years as a cabinetmaker I've found that it's rarely the big stroke of genius that makes the difference; rather, it's the avoidance of dumb mistakes. Simplifying cabinet designs and standardizing construction have made me feel a whole lot smarter. By making frameless cabinets, ordering the doors and drawer fronts from an outside vendor, and using production-oriented jigs, I've eliminated a lot of expensive router bits and stock preparation. Follow these guidelines and you'll be able to go from shop drawings to finished cabinets quickly and accurately, with a minimum number of expensive tools and mistakes.

## 1 Build the Boxes, but Buy the Doors

Making cabinet doors is tedious and doubles the amount of time needed to build a kitchen, so I prefer to let someone else do it. Before I start building cabinets, I order doors and drawer fronts from an outside supplier. They're usually ready (sanded and finished) by the time I've completed the cabinet cases. It's hard for me to meet the quality/price ratio that a shop can deliver.

IRON ON THE EDGING. A spring clamp keeps the edging in place while I work the iron from one end to the other.

TRIM ONE EDGE AT A TIME. I use only one side of my Virutex edge trimmer (www.virutex.com) at a time to ensure I am working with the grain.

## 2 Finish before You Start

Edgebanding and applying a finish are best done to big pieces, but not too big. My usual strategy is to rip 4×8 sheets of plywood into 2×8 pieces, a size that's easy to finish and move. You'll have to go back and add a little edgebanding after all the parts are cut, but working on 2×8 sheets first will get the work done faster.

Using the plywood as a ruler, I snap off a bunch of 97-in.-long strips of edgeband. With the help of a spring clamp, I balance a strip on the top edge of the plywood sheet so that it overhangs each end. With the iron on a hot (linen) setting, I tack down one end of the edgeband, then iron toward the other end. To ensure good adhesion, scuff the plywood edge beforehand with 80-grit sandpaper, then dust it clean with compressed air.

Edge trimmers normally trim both sides at once. That's fine for vinyl edging, but you'll get smoother results with wood if you show some respect for the grain. Pull the tool apart, and work one side at a time to avoid splits.

Before applying the varnish, it's a good idea to raise the grain with a damp sponge, then knock down the fuzzies with 220-grit sandpaper. This method speeds the process by requiring fewer coats to get a finer finish. I finish the banded edge and one side (the better-looking one) of each piece, which then becomes the inside of the cabinet. If you finish both sides, you're mostly wasting time on surfaces that you'll cover up later with adjacent cabinets, drawers, or end panels. After assembly, I finish any visible outer surfaces.

FINISH THE BEST SIDE. I only finish the best looking side of the plywood. The other side will not be visible when the cabinets are complete.

WHEN THE VARNISH HAS DRIED, I knock down the bumps before applying a second coat. Sandpaper works fine, but I like to smooth the finish with a cabinet scraper.

TIP. Single-edge razor blades make great scrapers for the edges.

CUT PLYWOOD EFFICIENTLY. To avoid making crosscuts in full-size sheets of plywood, I rip sheets lengthwise, then turn to crosscutting. My shopmade crosscut sled rides in the tablesaw's miter-gauge slots, making precise crosscutting easy.

## 3 Stick with Basic Dimensions

I begin the process by making a cutlist of all the parts I'll need (sides, tops, bottoms, backs, etc.) and note the dimensions both on the cutlist and on an unfinished end of the part (ballpoint ink will last). I use basic dimensions that divide well into a plywood panel. To account for the sawkerf, subtract ⅛ in. from the following sizes: 6 in. and 9 in. work well for drawers and toe-kick stock; 12 in., 16 in., and 18 in. work well for varying depths of upper-cabinet sides, tops, and bottoms; 24 in. is good for base cabinets.

## 4 Speed Assembly with Simple Joinery and a Low Table

Rarely do I rabbet cabinet backs or dado drawer bottoms. Instead, I fasten backs and bottoms directly to the edge of the plywood with polyurethane construction adhesive and nails or screws. When assembling, I use homemade corner blocks and a low assembly table to keep things square and at a comfortable working height.

Plywood cutoffs with square corners and lipped sides work well for clamping cabinet sides together or, as shown, for drawer assembly. I use a drawer side as a gauge to space the blocks properly. Then, with front and back standing, I wedge a side between to keep them steady while fastening the other side.

With the drawer sides assembled, use the drawer bottoms to rack and hold the boxes square. I prefer plywood over hardboard or medium-density fiberboard for the bottoms (and cabinet backs) because of its light weight, durability, and ability to hold fasteners.

KEEP IT SQUARE. Corner blocks made with shop scraps help to keep the parts aligned during assembly.

ADD THE BOTTOM. Once the sides are assembled the bottom holds the box square.

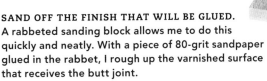

SAND OFF THE FINISH THAT WILL BE GLUED. A rabbeted sanding block allows me to do this quickly and neatly. With a piece of 80-grit sandpaper glued in the rabbet, I rough up the varnished surface that receives the butt joint.

DON'T CRAWL INTO A CABINET TO INSTALL DRAWER HARDWARE. Do it on a bench instead. With the cabinet on its side and the template wedged in place, I drill all the holes for the drawer slides with a cordless drill. Flip the cabinet and template over, align the front edge, and drill holes in the other side.

**DRAWER HARDWARE DRILLING TEMPLATE**

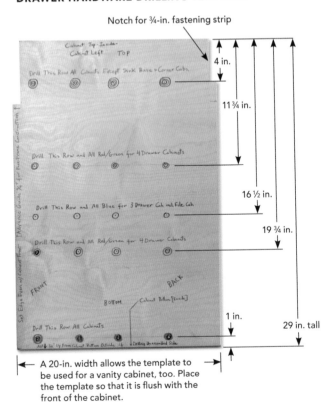

Notch for ¾-in. fastening strip

4 in.

11 ¾ in.

16 ½ in.

19 ¾ in.

1 in.

29 in. tall

A 20-in. width allows the template to be used for a vanity cabinet, too. Place the template so that it is flush with the front of the cabinet.

## 5 Use Drilling Templates

Because I think that base cabinets with shelves are a sin against common sense, I fill them with drawers or roll-out upgrades. But installing all that drawer hardware can be finicky business. I avoid a lot of mistakes by using a full-size template made from ¼-in. plywood or melamine. My template defines the positions of the holes for drawer slides in kitchen base cabinets (three- and four-drawer type), vanity cabinets, and file drawers, too. I simply color-code the holes to minimize mistakes.

For upper cabinets with adjustable shelves, I ensure accurate hole spacing by using a drilling template, which I made with a piece of melamine on a friend's line-boring machine. You also can buy a template from most woodworking stores. This template's spacing ensures consistency and allows you to take advantage of the European cabinetmaking system if you want to.

USE A CORDLESS DRILL TO PLACE SHELF HOLES ACCURATELY. Set this template against the bottom of the cabinet and work your way up. The template is symmetrical, but working from the bottom up avoids any problems caused by a cabinet side that may have been cut a bit shorter than the other.

**SHELF HOLE DRILLING TEMPLATE**

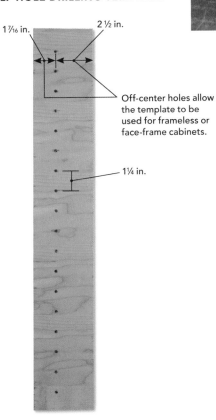

1 ⁷⁄₁₆ in.   2 ½ in.

Off-center holes allow the template to be used for frameless or face-frame cabinets.

1¼ in.

EASIER ACCESS. Install the cabinet backs last after drilling holes and installing the hardware. This approach boosts your screw-driving comfort zone by allowing access from front or back.

The cup hole must be close to the edge of the door or the door will rub against the cabinet when opened and closed. You almost can't get too close, but you certainly can get too far. About ⅛ in. will allow the door to overlay the cabinet frame fully without rubbing. With the cup hinge squarely in the hole, set one screw. This will ensure that all hinges are installed consistently.

**ALIGN THE HINGE STICK** with the top of the cabinet, drill pilot holes, and drive the baseplate screws. The bumpers ensure consistent setback on all the hinges.

Set the adjustable bumpers after the first set of hinges is in place and working happily.

Drill holes all the way through so that the stick can be used for left- or right-hinging and as a drilling guide.

Cup holes are drilled an equal distance from the end so that the stick can be flipped top or bottom.

## 6 Install Doors with a Hinge Stick

European-style hinges come in two pieces: a cup and a baseplate. The cup mounts to the door, and the baseplate mounts to the cabinet side. The two parts then snap or screw together. Because they're two-part hinges, it's crucial that the corresponding pieces line up, or they won't snap together. My hinge stick keeps the distance between baseplates and the setback from cabinet front consistent. To use it, insert cup hinges into the holes, and with the hinges in the closed position, screw the baseplates to the cabinet side. Test the operation of the door stick. If all's well, adjust the bumpered screws to the distance between the open door and the cabinet. Now you can install all the baseplates with the stick in the open position.

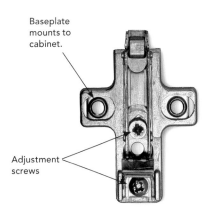

Baseplate mounts to cabinet.

Adjustment screws

Cup mounts to door.

**THE BEST WAY TO BORE THE CUP HOLES** is to use a 1³⁄₈-in. Forstner bit with a depth stop in a benchtop drill press. Set up a fence with reference marks to ensure consistent alignment. Without a benchtop drill press, the hinge stick can make a good drilling template if clamped to the door.

# A Faster, Easier Approach to Custom Cabinets

BY MIKE MAINES

When designed and constructed properly, built-in cabinets can bring both style and storage to many parts of a home. Over the years, I've refined my approach to constructing cabinets to decrease the time and tools it takes to build them while ensuring their strength and good looks. I used my technique to build the Douglas-fir kitchen island featured here for my home, but I've followed the same process to make stain- and paint-grade kitchen cabinets, bookcases, linen cabinets, pantries, desks, bathroom vanities, and storage cubbies.

## Your Shop Is Where You Make It

The beauty of this system is that the setup is simple and doesn't rely on the space or tools found in big cabinet shops. Being able to set up shop in a driveway, a garage, or a small room has always been helpful in keeping my work on schedule.

The tools you need to construct these cabinets are likely sitting in the back of your truck. For cutting components to size, you need a miter saw, a portable tablesaw, a circular saw, an edge guide to cut sheet goods safely, and a portable thickness planer. To fasten the carcase and face frames together, you need a 16-gauge or 18-gauge finish nailer, a screw gun, a pocket-screw jig (www.kregtool.com; www. pennstateind.com), a bunch of screws, and some glue.

## A Hybrid Design Makes Face-Frame Cabinets Better

Cabinets are typically designed in one of two ways: frameless or with face frames. Each has its merits. Face-frame cabinets are traditional and strong, and they can be scribed to fit seamlessly against a wall. Frameless cabinets are quicker to put together and can be used in conjunction with adjustable, hidden, and now soft-close hinges.

I've done a lot of historically informed work, and frameless boxes just don't provide the appeal of face-frame cabinets with inset doors. Although frameless cabinets allow a bit more space inside, their end panels tend to look tacked-on, crown molding is hard to detail properly, and filler strips are heavily relied on during installation. I use the benefits of both styles by building a hybrid cabinet. Flushing the inside of the carcase to the inside of the face frame allows me to use hardware designed for frameless cabinets while still providing the traditional look, ease of installation, and strength of face-frame construction.

CUT ALL THE FACE-FRAME COMPONENTS AT ONCE. When milling 1×6 face-frame material to size, I like to fine-tune its final width with a planer, not a tablesaw. I use a tablesaw to square all boards with rounded edges. Then I rip the face-frame stock ⅛ in. wider than I need on a tablesaw. Finally, I remove the last ⅛ in. with a planer. The planer produces more precise dimensions and smoother cuts.

PLANE SIMILAR PARTS TOGETHER. Instead of planing each board individually, plane all the end stiles, then inner stiles, and then rails to their exact width.

CHOP TO LENGTH. Armed with a fence and a stop made of scrap material and a cut list, chop all the face-frame material to its precise length. Stack all the material to make a complete face frame.

# GOOD PROPORTIONS ARE NO ACCIDENT

**ALTHOUGH MY BUILT-IN CABINETS** are assembled easily, there's no guarantee they'll look good in a home. A cabinet constructed with wacky proportions won't look or function as well as it should. To start, make a scale drawing on paper of each piece you intend to build. Having this reference on hand will give you a clear idea of what you're building and will help you create a detailed cutlist. I follow a few basic rules when it comes to designing cabinets.

- Built-in cabinets that will be used as workstations generally have countertops 36 in. above the floor, so boxes should be built to a height of 34½ in.

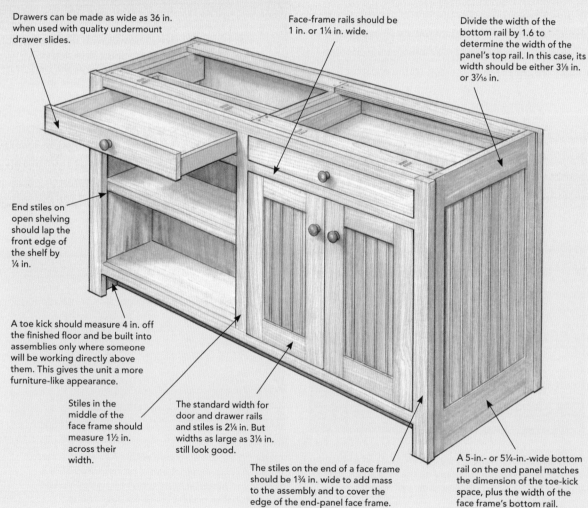

Drawers can be made as wide as 36 in. when used with quality undermount drawer slides.

Face-frame rails should be 1 in. or 1¼ in. wide.

Divide the width of the bottom rail by 1.6 to determine the width of the panel's top rail. In this case, its width should be either 3⅛ in. or 3⁷⁄₁₆ in.

End stiles on open shelving should lap the front edge of the shelf by ¼ in.

A toe kick should measure 4 in. off the finished floor and be built into assemblies only where someone will be working directly above them. This gives the unit a more furniture-like appearance.

Stiles in the middle of the face frame should measure 1½ in. across their width.

The standard width for door and drawer rails and stiles is 2¼ in. But widths as large as 3¼ in. still look good.

The stiles on the end of a face frame should be 1¾ in. wide to add mass to the assembly and to cover the edge of the end-panel face frame.

A 5-in.- or 5¼-in.-wide bottom rail on the end panel matches the dimension of the toe-kick space, plus the width of the face frame's bottom rail.

to 35 in., depending on the thickness of the countertop. Cabinets that aren't task oriented can be any size and are built without toe kicks. I distinguish these units by building the bottom rail taller or shorter than the house's baseboard. When in doubt of any proportions, I use the golden rectangle, a shape 1.6 times as high as it is wide. I also find the widths of components by dividing similar members by 1.6, as done with the end-panel rails.

- When multiple cabinet boxes are lined up in a row, they appear more fitted when tied together with a single face frame. I connect the boxes by hiding a screw behind each door hinge. You can make all the face-frame components the same size, but that can make the rails look fat and the end stiles look skinny. Instead, I like to adjust their widths (see the drawing on the facing page) so that the built-in looks more balanced.
- Doors should always be taller than they are wide and should never exceed 20 in. in width; otherwise they project too far into a space when opened. Even an 18-in.-wide door can be too large on certain units. Drawers should be left with a flat face when they're shorter than 4½ in., which is typical, and can be detailed to match frame-and-panel doors when they're taller.

## Screws, Glue, and Quality Hardware Hold It Together

Traditionally, face-frame cabinets are constructed with dadoes, grooves, dowels, or mortise-and-tenon joinery to lock together each component. These techniques create strong assemblies but require a good bit of time.

I assemble face frames with fine-thread, 1¼-in. square-drive washer-head pocket screws and yellow glue. I tack the carcases together with finish nails and then drive 1⅝-in. drywall screws for strength. I've used drywall screws for years and have never had a cabinet fail, but it's important to use stronger screws when attaching a cabinet to the wall.

**ASSEMBLE THE FACE FRAMES FIRST.** I build all the face frames before I build their corresponding boxes. This not only saves room on the job site but also allows me to use the face frames for reference when a dimension comes into question during carcase construction. To start, dry-fit the face-frame components so their grain and color look best. Mark the boards to show their orientation in the assembly and where they'll be pocket screwed.

 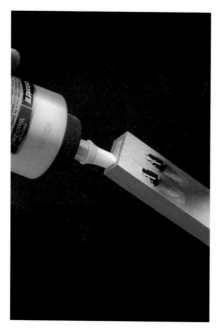 

**A POCKET-HOLE JIG MAKES ASSEMBLY EASY.** Drill two pocket holes in the end of each rail and each inner stile.

**SQUEEZE THE GRAIN TO ELIMINATE SPLITTING.** Put a bit of wood glue on the board end before securing a locking C-clamp so that it exerts equal pressure on the grain of each component. The clamp should be placed in line with the pocket hole being screwed.

**QUALITY CONTROL.** Check to be sure that every component is aligned and secured properly before building subsequent frames. Accuracy here is crucial because the dimensions of the face frame might be used as a reference when building the boxes.

JIG TIP. I make a simple jig out of thin medium-density fiberboard (MDF) to orient shelf pinholes 1½ in. from the front and back of the box. I usually place the first hole 12 in. off the bottom of the box and drill holes in 1½-in. increments above and below.

BUILD THE BOXES. Box assembly is a relatively straightforward process. Before the sides of the boxes are fastened together, though, I drill pocket holes and the holes for shelving pins. Please note that full sheets of plywood should never be cut on a tablesaw. Instead, use a straightedge clamped to the sheet's surface and a circular saw with a fine-toothed alternate top bevel (ATB) sawblade.

DRILL POCKET HOLES IN GROUPS OF TWO. When preparing the sides of the carcase that will be joined with the face frame, drill two holes instead of one for each connection point. This extra step will come in handy when attaching the face frames.

Beyond box strength, cabinets are often measured by the quality of their hardware. The best hinge for this hybrid system is a 32 mm cup hinge made by Blum (www.blum.com) or Mepla (www.mepla-alfit .com). Adjustable, self-closing, and quick to install, they are usually my first choice. In more historically accurate work when a visible hinge is preferred or when I don't want a hinge to intrude on storage space, I like to use Cliffside's 2-in. butt hinges (www.cliffsideind.com). I use a trim router to mortise the door for a single leaf and don't mortise the face frame at all, which helps provide just the right reveal between the door and the face frame.

I've used all three types of drawer slides in my cabinets, but when I have a choice, I opt for the Blum Tandem, an undermount full-extension unit that is forgiving to install and smooth to operate.

For adjustable shelves, I like to drill groups of three to five holes where I think the shelf should be.

TACK AND SCREW TO-GETHER THE BOX PARTS. Nailing the box with 16-gauge finish nails makes it easier to keep pieces in place while they're locked together with 1⅝-in. drywall screws.

This allows some adjustability while avoiding the factory-made look of a continuous row of holes. Often, I use paddle-type supports installed in a 5 mm hole. For heavy-duty applications, such as a bookshelf, I like an L-shaped pin in a ¼-in. hole.

## Get Doors and Drawer Fronts That Fit the Second Time

I order or build doors and drawer fronts before the built-ins are complete so I can finish the job quickly. To be sure they fit the way I want them to, with the perfect reveal, I have them built to the exact size of the face-frame opening written on my plans. Once on site, I fit them tight into their openings. I reduce their size on all sides a heavy ¹⁄₁₆ in. by taking measurements from the face frame, not the door or drawer front itself, and rip them on the tablesaw.

**SUPPORT THE BOX AND THE DRAWER SLIDES.** On top of each box and below each drawer, ¾-in. plywood crosspieces add strength, a place to connect the face frame's top rail, and a surface to attach countertops and undermount drawer slides.

**ATTACH THE FACE FRAMES TO THE BOXES.** A face frame can be nailed to a box with 16-gauge finish nails. However, the holes still need to be filled, and the gun can scuff the face-frame surface. Another way to attach face frames is with biscuit joinery, a solid solution, but one that demands a lot of time and a massive arsenal of clamps. By attaching the face frame with pocket screws, I get an immediate, permanent connection while leaving the face of the cabinet clear.

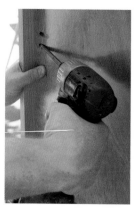

**PICK A HOLE, BUT NOT JUST ANY HOLE.** Although I drilled groups of two pocket holes in the box, only one hole in each set needs to be screwed. The face frame should flush with the inside of the box perfectly, but if it doesn't, having multiple holes gives you the flexibility to push and pull the face frame into alignment.

# DRESS UP AN EXPOSED END PANEL

**BUILT-IN CABINETS** usually have their sides buried in a wall. Sometimes, however, the sides and even the back are exposed to public view. I detail these areas to hide pocket holes in a couple of ways.

On my kitchen island, I used a stock of reclaimed Douglas-fir edge and center bead that had been collecting dust in my garage for years. I simply filled the face-frame opening with the boards, attaching them with an 18-gauge pin nailer. Held tight against the carcase, the ¾-in.-thick face frame would leave a ¼-in. reveal where it meets the end stiles of the front face frame. So I furred out the end panel with ³⁄₁₆-in. plywood strips to reduce the size of the reveal.

If I'm not going to use bead board on a built-in, I fill the face frame with ½-in. plywood to create a flat recessed panel. Alternatively, I cover the entire side of the carcase with a sheet of ¼-in. plywood that can be stained or painted to match the wood I've used, then glue and nail the face frame to it.

**COVER YOUR TRACKS.** To hide pocket holes and screws used to assemble the cabinet, wrap exposed faces with a decorative material, such as stain- or paint-grade plywood, bead board, or edge and center bead.

# A New Approach to Classic Cabinets

BY MIKE MAINES

The room in the southwest corner of our 1830s Greek revival is by far the fanciest in the house, with its tall baseboards and door casing with flat planes meeting at an angle instead of the more common rounded field. Even the windows are fancy—at least by the standards of rural Maine—with the casings running to the floor and a flat panel under each that is finished to match the walls. The existing fireplace surround, however, was not very attractive.

My wife and I appreciate the history of our house, but we have no desire to live in a museum. So we decided it was time to design and build a fireplace surround, complete with a pair of bookcase cabinets, which would be honest to the spirit of the house but updated with a slightly modern feel.

Over the years I've refined my approach to building cabinets without the luxury of a fully stocked cabinetry shop, so I knew this was a project I could tackle on site.

## Modernizing the Style

The design process involved a lot of sketches and scribbles, but it breaks down simply: The fireplace surround is proportioned to be stocky and proud, just like the house. The flanking bookcases have clean lines and flush surfaces. Meant to evoke clas-

sical columns, they look traditional without being fussy. The two pilasters (the legs of the mantel) sit on plinth blocks. The frieze (or lintel) projects beyond the pilasters by ¼ in., just like the plinth blocks. The mantel shelf is 1¼ in. thick, just like most of the other horizontal components, with a flat, angled molding supporting the shelf. After considering many options for the supporting molding, we settled on a simple, angled crown. I realized later that this matches the crown molding on the house's exterior, which gave me confidence that I was on the right track.

## Start with the Right Materials

Most of this project makes use of two materials: solid ¾-in. (nominal 4/4) D4S (dressed on four sides) poplar lumber and ¾-in. veneer-core birch plywood. Poplar is my go-to material for paint-grade trim and cabinetry. It is hard, stable, affordable, relatively knot-free, and usually straight-grained. It is also easy to work with both hand tools and power tools, and it's readily available here in the Northeast.

For carcases, I like to use a good grade of veneer-core plywood. When choosing between plywood panels, my first decision involves the quality of the face veneer, which in order from best to worst is graded AA, A, B, C, D, and E. Here, I used plywood

# FACE FRAMES COME FIRST

EVERYBODY WANTS TO BUILD THE BOXES FIRST and then add the face frames. Even if you have the room to work around a bunch of boxes while you try to mill, assemble, and install the face frames, why bother? Maybe you like to build each cabinet separately from start to finish. Good luck making a living with that approach. To make money, you need to be fast. Build the face frames first, then set them aside.

HIDDEN SCREWS. After marking the rail positions on the stiles, fasten each rail with at least two pocket screws. For wider rails, use more screws, and make sure to favor the outer edges of the boards to help prevent cupping. Once fastened, the frame can be sanded smooth on both sides and set aside.

SHELF-PIN HOLES ON THE CHEAP. Instead of buying a jig, mark and drill the desired pin layout into ¼-in. plywood. Clamp the template along the edge of the side pieces, and use a self-centering shelf-pin drill bit to bore the holes.

PAIRS OF POCKETS. The face frame is screwed to the case sides through pocket holes drilled in pairs. Use only one hole out of each pair; if the first screw pushes parts out of alignment, you have a second option right there.

**ASSEMBLY SHOULD LEAVE ROOM FOR ADJUSTMENT. If you've cut all the parts correctly, the face frame and the plywood should line up perfectly. If they don't line up first start with nails. Tack the plywood box together with 15-ga. or 16-ga. finish nails. It will be a little floppy, but that's a good thing at this point.**

**HIDDEN ATTACHMENT. After nailing the box together, align the long sides of the face frame to the cabinet, and fasten them with pocket-hole screws. The screws will be covered by end panels after installation.**

with a grade-B face, which is better than shop-grade plywood but not the fully grain-matched product that is typical for stain-grade work. The back side of the plywood can be graded as 1, 2, 3, or 4. I chose a grade-1 back, which is nearly as nice as the grade-B face except that it can have more filled knots. I like birch for the face veneer because it has a discreet but still slightly apparent grain pattern, yet it costs a little less than other veneers. I prefer veneer-core plywood over MDF-core plywood because it's lighter and the dust is not as nasty. Finally, I use ¾-in. plywood for carcases because it's thick enough to accept screws and pocket-hole joinery.

The cabinet backs for this project were made from red birch coated with a clear oil finish. Not just any red birch (which in the Northeast, at least, usually refers to the heartwood of a yellow birch or sometimes a paper birch), the boards in this project were cut from logs recovered from the bottom of Maine's Moosehead Lake. The boards I chose have tight grain, rich color, lots of character, and a great story to go with them.

To be true to the house, we decided to use traditional butt hinges for the doors, albeit installed in my slightly nontraditional manner, which allows for some adjustment if the doors warp a bit.

TAP IT INTO ALIGN-
MENT. Use a hammer
and block to tap the
tops, bottoms, and
any fixed shelves into
alignment, then fasten
them with pocket
screws.

SECURE IT WITH
SCREWS. After
everything is aligned,
fasten through the
sides of the cabinet
with 1⅝-in. screws.
Shorter screws won't
hold well, and longer
screws may lead to
splits.

SOLID BACKS MEAN EXTRA STEPS. After
slotting the edge of each back board to
receive a ¼ -in.-thick plywood spline, fasten
the boards with screws in a combination of
countersunk and slotted holes to allow for
seasonal movement.

## Traditional Work Can Still Use Modern Joinery

Although I considered using my Festool® Domino
joiner to build the face frames, I ultimately opted
for the speed and simplicity of pocket-screw joinery
on these parts. I like to add a dab of glue to the
joints; end-grain gluing only has one-tenth the
strength of edge-grain gluing, but I think it contrib-
utes to the joint staying tight and not telegraphing
through the paint.

For joining the plywood carcases, I used my no-
fuss, adjustable method in which each box is constructed loosely and then tweaked as needed to fit
the more-rigid face frame. I have tried every possible
way to join face frames to carcases; my go-to method
for paint-grade work is to glue the face frames on,
tacking them in place with 18-ga. brad nails. The
downside to that method is that the filled nail holes
sometimes telegraph through the paint. Because our
new house has an intermittently wet basement, I ex-

pect significant fluctuations in humidity, so I chose
my "high-end" system of attaching the face frames
with pocket screws.

The backs presented an unusual challenge. I typically use plywood because it's self-squaring and
easy to attach with screws or narrow-crown staples.
But solid wood needs room for seasonal movement.
I bought the red birch planks rough-sawn, then
milled them to ¾ in. thick, straightened them with a
track saw, and grooved their edges with a router. The
groove was sized to accept plywood splines that hold
everything in plane but still allow the solid boards
to expand and contract. I drilled pilot holes in the
perimeter and the center of each board, but to allow
for expansion, I used the Domino to create elongated
slots at each edge of the wider boards. All the boards
are attached to the carcase with bugle-headed cabinet screws.

TRIM THE FAT. Use a track saw to remove as much wood as possible without reaching the scribe line. Back-cutting at a 30-degree bevel makes the hand-planing easier.

FINISH WITH CARE. For a simple scribe, use a block plane to shave up to the line. Complicated scribes may need a jigsaw or an angle grinder with a sanding disk.

SCRIBE FOR A TIGHT FIT. I usually leave a stile that will butt against a wall or other finished surface ¼ in. to ¾ in. wider than necessary so that it can be scribed for a perfect fit. After marking the scribe in place, I lay the cabinet flat on its back so that I can cut to the line and then finish the edge with a block plane.

To attach the cabinets to the wall, I used #10 wood screws with finishing washers, placed to lower their visibility once the shelves were installed and loaded with books. I shimmed the cabinets adequately at the floor, so the screws in the wall aren't bearing any weight.

The cabinets and the trim are both finished with Sherwin-Williams' Multi-Purpose Latex Primer and topcoated with two coats of Benjamin Moore's Advance waterborne alkyd paint in a semigloss finish. I had planned to use my Graco airless spray gun for the primer coat only, because I think a brushed finish is more appropriate for an old house like ours, but once I went through the effort to mask everything off, I decided to spray the two topcoats as well. The finish came out great, and I highly recommend the paint, which flows out better and dries harder than regular latex paints. My wife and I love the way the new fireplace surround ties the room together.

# DOORS THAT BREAK ALL THE RULES

**A TYPICAL CABINET DOOR** consists of a framework of rails and stiles—usually assembled with cope-and-stick, mortise-and-tenon, or other joinery—with grooved edges that capture a panel. The frame holds the panel but allows it to expand and contract seasonally. For this project, I tried a new technique.

I used the Festool Domino tool to cut slots on all edges of the ¾-in. plywood panels, rails, and stiles, and on the ends of the rails. After cutting a rabbet around the panel to create a reveal, I glued the panels right in their frames.

**MARK TO AVOID MIX-UPS.** Arrange the door parts with their finished sides facing up. Draw a triangle in the center of the panel, then mark each stile and rail with the corresponding portion of the triangle that matches its position relative to the panel. Mark the same number in each triangle so that you know the grouping and orientation of each part.

**SLOTS, NOT BISCUITS.** In terms of layout and use, operating the Domino is very similar to operating a biscuit joiner. Mark both pieces where they will join, dial in the height and depth, and plunge the tool into each piece to create a matching slot.

**A RABBETED SHADOW-LINE.** To disguise the joint between panel and door frame, and to create a nice reveal, rabbet the edges of each panel on the finished side. Hit the rabbets with spackle, primer, and a light sanding before assembly.

**GLUE AND CLAMP.** After inserting glue and tenons into the edges of the plywood panel, dab glue into the tenon holes of the stiles, rails, and along their edges. Position the rails first, repeat the process for the stiles, and then clamp everything together. Using a straightedge as a guide, adjust the position of the clamps to ensure that the doors are flat.

# THE TRICKS TO QUICK BUTT HINGES

I CHOSE THE BH2A SERIES OF BUTT HINGES from Cliffside Industries because I like the adjustment offered by their slotted holes. When working with these butt hinges, I like to follow two tricks I learned from a local cabinetmaker. First, mortise the door only; the other leaf of the hinge will create a nice reveal. Second, don't bother with stopped mortises; cut them right from the front of the door through to the back.

**SITE-MADE MORTISE JIG.** Plywood scraps are all that's needed to make a custom hinge jig. A router with a flush-bearing bit rides the jig to cut the through mortise.

**PLAN FOR ADJUSTABILITY.** Place the hinges with the horizontal holes on the door and the vertical holes on the cabinet, and you'll have some room for adjusting.

**HANG AND ADJUST IN PLACE.** With the hinges in place on the cabinet doors, hold the doors in position while you transfer the hinge locations to the face frame. Attach the door, and tweak as needed for a perfect close.

# Making an Arched Cabinet Face-Frame Rail

BY GARY STRIEGLER

For a recent cabinet design I included a curved rail across the top. I like this face-frame feature because the curve gives the cabinet a nice visual uplift. It's also fairly easy to make. The hardest work is drawing the design; the rest is just cutting stock.

I start with a full sheet of medium-density fiberboard (MDF) or plywood laid on a pair of sawhorses. The sheet becomes a chalkboard on which I draw the cabinet's face frame in full scale. I use a set of trammel points to establish the radius. Because I'm only drawing, I can fool with the radius until I get something that looks good. Because the curve forms the cabinet's top rail, I also need to leave enough room for crown molding.

When the arc looks right, I mount a router base on a narrow piece of plywood that acts as a trammel, clamp the upper-rail blank on the table, and cut a shallow arc. I then rough out the curve with a jigsaw and finish the cut with a flush-trim bit. A couple of quick passes over the cut with a random-orbit sander readies the rail for installation.

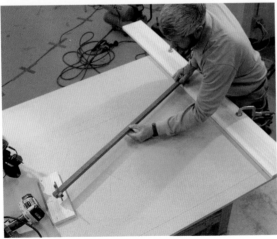

**BLOCK UP THE PIVOT POINT.** When the arc's proportion is right, attach a small plywood block at the centerpoint. Redraw the centerpoint on the block, then drill a small pilot hole to mark the pivot point for the router trammel.

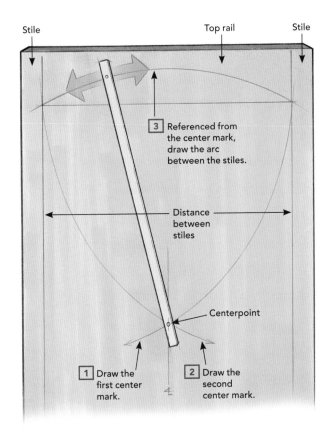

Stile

Top rail

Stile

**3** Referenced from the center mark, draw the arc between the stiles.

Distance between stiles

Centerpoint

**1** Draw the first center mark.

**2** Draw the second center mark.

## PLOTTING A RADIUS

To determine the radius for a curved rail, draw the cabinet's face frame in full scale on a sheet of MDF, plywood, or cardboard. Start with a set of trammel points set to the distance between the stiles.

**1** Anchor one trammel end at the intersection of the stile and top rail. Then draw a center mark below.

**2** Repeat from the opposite side to create a center mark that determines the new anchor point for the trammel.

**3** Without changing the trammel points, draw an arc from this centerpoint that connects the two stiles. If the arc has too deep or too shallow a radius, lengthen or shorten the distance between the trammel points and repeat the process.

# AN ESSENTIAL DESIGN TOOL

I USE A SET OF ADJUSTABLE TRAMMEL POINTS to determine and draw radii. The points can be fastened to any length of material ¾ in. thick or less. Each set is equipped with two steel pins, one of which can be replaced with a pencil. Trammel points can be found in most lumberyards and home centers. The pair I use are manufactured by General®. You also can make a trammel by driving a screw into one end of a length of board and fastening a pencil to the other end.

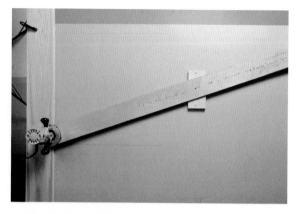

PUT A ROUTER ON THE TRAMMEL. Attach a router base to the end of a 6-in.-wide strip of plywood that's a bit longer than the radius (top left). Clamp the face frame's top-rail stock to the MDF, and align it to the drawing (above). Use a ½-in.- or ¾-in.-dia. straight bit in the router, and attach the router trammel to the plywood block with a single screw so that the outer edge of the bit cuts the radius. Set the bit depth to ¼ in. and make the cut (left), moving left to right.

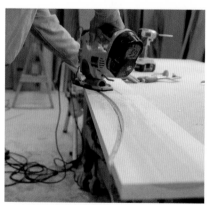

A ROUGH CUT WORKS. Next, remove most of the waste with a jigsaw, making sure to stay ⅛ in. or so away from the finished line.

CLEAN IT UP. Exchange the straight bit for a flush-trim bit. Flip over the rail and clamp it down so that the radius is hanging over the edge of the worksurface. The bit's bearing should be riding on the first router cut. The radius can be dressed with a final router pass and sanded.

# Making Raised-Panel Doors on a Tablesaw

BY REX ALEXANDER

Cabinet shops that turn out raised-panel doors rely on heavy-duty shapers and cutters or, at the very least, a router-table setup that includes a range of expensive bits. You also can make raised-panel doors with a portable tablesaw. The doors I build this way often are referred to as Shaker style. The vertical stiles and horizontal rails that make up the frame have square rather than contoured edges. The center panel, which floats in the frame, is a raised piece of solid wood (a flat piece of plywood also works).

Whether you make a single door or many using this technique, you'll need a stacked dado set in addition to a finish-cutting combination blade. For best results, the wood you use to build doors should be free of knots, warps, twists, and checks. I frequently use poplar (shown here) for doors that will be painted.

### A BASIC CABINET DOOR

Stiles (vertical frame members) join rails (horizontal frame members) with a tongue-and-groove joint. The frame is glued together, but the raised panel floats in the groove. A ⅛-in. clearance space around the panel provides room for expansion.

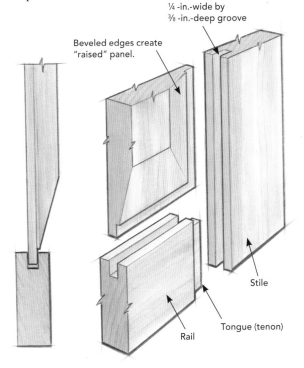

¼ -in.-wide by ⅜ -in.-deep groove

Beveled edges create "raised" panel.

Stile

Tongue (tenon)

Rail

CUT THE GROOVE.
A stacked dado set replaces the tablesaw blade to groove the stiles and rails.

## Use a Dado Head to Groove the Stiles and Rails

Replace the tablesaw blade with a stacked dado set (see the sidebar at right). The cutting width should be ¼ in. Adjust the cutting height to ⅜ in. Position the saw's rip fence so that the groove will be centered in the frame members. Cutting test grooves in scrap stock (the same thickness as the stiles and rails) is a smart idea to assure you that the setup is right.

## Cut Each Tongue in One Pass

Each rail end needs a tongue or short tenon that fits snugly in the grooved stile. You can cut away the waste on each side of the tongue by inserting steel

washers between the dado cutters. The space you create needs to match the planned thickness of the tongue. Cut test pieces, adding or subtracting washers as necessary until the tongue fits snugly. The thin washers that come with most stacked dado sets help to fine-tune the fit.

**SPLIT THE DADO HEAD TO CUT TONGUES IN THE RAILS.** Insert steel washers between the dado cutters to cut away the waste on each side of the tongue.

To cut tongues safely and accurately, clamp the rails to a sliding cradle. As shown in the photos at right, my cradle consists of a vertical guide block fastened to a horizontal runner. The runner slides on the top edge of an auxiliary rip fence.

## Bevel the Panel, Trim the Edges, and Assemble the Door

Size the panel as shown in the drawing on p. 69 so that there will be ⅛ in. of clearance space around the panel edges after the door is assembled. Adjust the tablesaw's bevel angle to 15 degrees. Adjust the rip fence so that it's ¼ in. from the blade, the same distance as the thickness of the panel groove. Raise the blade so that the teeth just penetrate the opposite side of the panel. Now you're ready to make the bevel cuts that will create the raised edges.

To fit properly in the grooved frame, the panel edges should have a uniform thickness instead of being beveled. Replace the sawblade with a ¼ -in.- wide dado head. Then place the panel upside down on the saw table and raise the dado head so that it will remove the beveled edge, leaving a flat edge of the correct thickness. Position the rip fence ¹⁄₁₆ in.

**CUT THE TONGUES.** The rails are clamped to a sliding cradle which consists of a vertical guide block fastened to a horizontal runner that slides on the top edge of an auxiliary rip fence.

**RAISE THE PANEL EDGES.** The author makes bevel cuts to create the raised panel edges. To hold the panel upright, he clamps a runner block to the panel so that the block will be guided by the top edge of the rip fence, as shown in the top right photo.

**FLATTEN THE OUTER EDGES.** (left) The panel edges need to have a uniform thickness to fit properly in the frame. A ¼ -in. dado head is used to remove the bevel.

**TEST FIT, SAND, AND ASSEMBLE.** (bottom) The author dry fits the panel to make sure every part fits without being forced. 100-grit sandpaper wrapped around a sanding block can narrow any problem panel edges.

away from the dado head; spin the blade by hand to make sure it doesn't contact the fence. Then turn on the saw and guide the panel against the rip fence to flatten its edges.

Do a dry run through the assembly process to make sure the panel fits into the stile-and-rail frame without being forced. If necessary, you can narrow the panel edge with some 100-grit sandpaper wrapped around a sanding block. When the fit is right, give the panel a final sanding. Use 120-grit sandpaper if the door will be painted, and 220-grit if you plan to use stain or clear finish. When you glue up the door, take care to spread glue only on the tongue-and-groove joints between frame members. Use bar or pipe clamps to keep the joints tight until the glue dries.

# Cabinet Openings with Applied Beading

BY GARY STRIEGLER

Kitchens are usually the crown jewels of the custom houses I build. The detail requested most often for these kitchens is beaded trim around cabinet-door and drawer openings (see the photo at right). Whether paint grade or stain grade, this distinctive element can raise the style of any kitchen to a higher level—and it's surprisingly simple to execute.

## A Bit Cuts the Bead

I've used beaded molding to embellish many different trim details, from exterior window trim to interior door casing. Beads come in a variety of shapes and configurations. The most common bead, such as the one used for these cabinet openings, is a small half-round profile separated from the main body of the face frame by a narrow, flat section similar to a sawkerf.

A bead can be cut directly into the face frame of the cabinet or into the edge of the trim, but I've found that it's much easier to use the bead as an applied molding. The flat part of the profile is recessed behind the cabinet face to make an invisible joint between the bead and the face frame.

To make beaded molding, start by chucking a beading bit in a router. Beading bits are readily available from a number of suppliers; I got mine from

Woodcraft® Supply (www.woodcraft.com). Beading bits come in different diameters to fit the scale of a particular job (see the photo on p. 74). For beaded trim on kitchen cabinets, I use a bearing-guided bit that cuts a ¼-in.-dia. bead. Because only a small amount of wood has to be removed, a compact laminate trimmer cuts the bead with easy handling and maximum control (see the left photo on p. 75).

Inset cup hinges allow you to adjust the doors in every direction. The result is an even space between the doors and the bead. A hinge backer glued and nailed behind the bead provides a place to attach the mounting plate for the hinge.

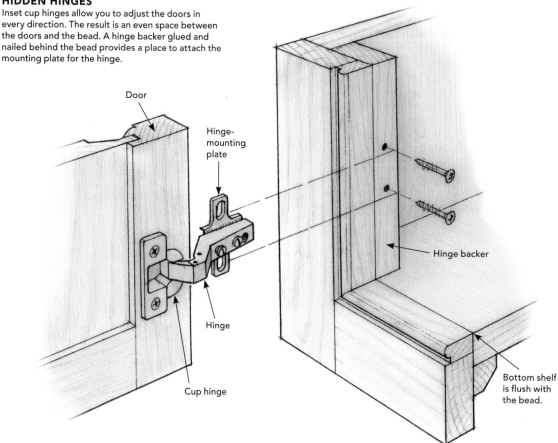

Door

Hinge-mounting plate

Hinge

Cup hinge

Hinge backer

Bottom shelf is flush with the bead.

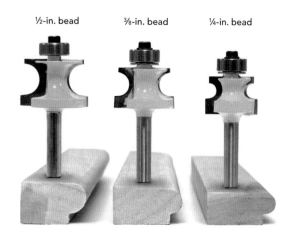

½-in. bead   ⅜-in. bead   ¼-in. bead

**BITS FOR DIFFERENT BEADS.** Sold by bead diameter, different-size beading bits work for moldings of every scale, from cabinets to door trim.

After cutting a bead on both edges of a length of flat stock, rip the molding from the board in two passes on the tablesaw (see the drawing on the facing page). The first pass cuts the molding to the width of the frame stock (see the center photo on the facing page). The second cut is adjacent to the flat section of the profile and sets the height of the molding (see the right photo on the facing page).

## Raise the Bottom Shelf

I build face-frame cabinets for beaded openings the same way as any other cabinet, except that I raise the bottom shelf an amount equal to the thickness of the beaded molding. The molding then continues the plane of the bottom shelf. Cut and install the shortest molding pieces first (in this case, the sides) using glue and brads. A hinge backer nails onto the same plane as the inside face of the molding.

# ONE BEAD, TWO RIPS

AFTER A BEAD HAS BEEN ROUTED into the opposite edges of flat stock ⌞1⌟, the first cut rips the molding to the same width as the face-frame thickness ⌞2⌟. The second cut rips the molding to the edge of the shoulder (the flat section of the profile) ⌞3⌟.

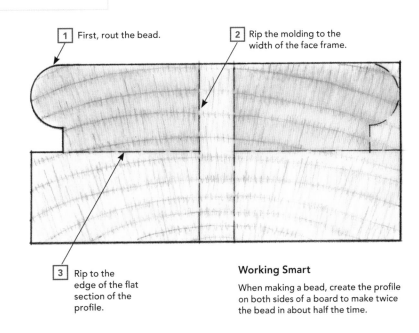

⌞1⌟ First, rout the bead.

⌞2⌟ Rip the molding to the width of the face frame.

⌞3⌟ Rip to the edge of the flat section of the profile.

**Working Smart**

When making a bead, create the profile on both sides of a board to make twice the bead in about half the time.

⌞1⌟ Rout the bead.

⌞2⌟ Rip the width.

⌞3⌟ Rip the thickness.

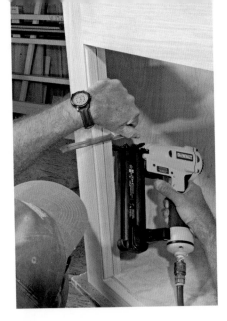

SIDE BEADS GO IN FIRST. If the sides are the shortest, they're the first pieces to go around the opening (far left). A hinge backer glues and nails flush with the beaded molding (left).

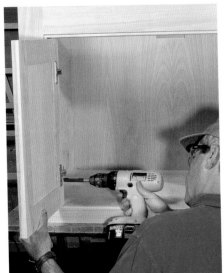

CUP HINGES GUARANTEE A PERFECT FIT. With the door held in its installed position, drill pilot holes for hinge-mounting plates and screw the plates to their hinge backers. Then mount the doors and adjust the hinges.

BEND EASES INSTALLATION. Rather than force a tightly fitting molding into place, insert one end and bend the molding slightly. The other end of the molding then can slide into position. Releasing the bend springs the molding into place for a perfect fit without smearing the glue.

The top and bottom moldings go in next. Cut each piece to the exact length, but rather than trying to force the molding into place, smearing the glue and making a mess in the process, insert one end and bend the piece slightly before pushing it into place (see the bottom left photo above). The bend virtually shortens the molding so that it slides into place without being forced.

## Adjustable Hinges for a Perfect Fit

There are two hinge options with beaded openings. For stain-grade work I like to use offset hinges with exposed decorative barrels. But for paint-grade cabinets I usually mount the doors with inset European cup hinges. They adjust in and out as well as up and down, making any carpenter with a screwdriver look like a pro.

When I get the doors in place, I simply tweak the hinges until the gap between the doors and the beaded molding as well as the space between the doors is perfectly even. If I've made everything square, the cabinet with its beaded opening is ready to install in the kitchen.

# Face Frames with a Mitered Integral Bead

BY BRENT BENNER

I was lucky to begin my woodworking career by apprenticing in two small New England cabinet shops. Each cabinetmaker had his own style, but they had one thing in common. If their shop was going to produce quality pieces efficiently and turn a profit, then accuracy and craftsmanship were key. One detail we used was the bead that ran along the perimeter of a door or a face frame. This detail softens the edge but creates a sharp shadowline.

There are two types of bead. An applied bead is typically shaped on the edge of a board, ripped off, then applied with glue and brads. An integral bead is shaped on the face-frame stock itself.

Both processes have advantages. I use an applied bead when I'm adding a bead to arched or curved stock. An applied bead is also the way to go if a drawer front rather than a face frame needs a bead. Any other time, I can work more efficiently by mill-

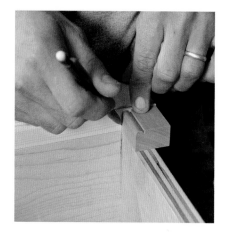

**DRY BISCUITS HELP LAYOUT.** I cut the face-frame rails and stiles to length, then start the layout with the outside stiles. I use dry biscuits to align them with the inside edge of the carcase (right), then use a scrap piece to mark the bead miter locations (above).

ing an integral bead. There are no nail holes to fill, which is important when working with stain-grade materials, and it's easier to flush the face frame and the interior of the cabinet.

I profile the stock on the flat with a horizontal router setup and featherboards; it seems to produce more consistent results than a vertical setup. For most cabinet face frames, I use a ¼-in.-dia. Jesada® edge-beading bit (www.jesada.com) with the guide bearing removed.

After cutting the rails and stiles to length, I biscuit (dry, no glue yet) the pieces to the cabinet boxes and work the mitered cuts in place. I start with the two outside stiles, marking and cutting the miter locations with a scrap and marking knife or fine pencil (see the left photo above). Then I mark, cut, and place the interior rails (and stiles, if any). Once I've gotten everything to fit, I remove the pieces and pocket-screw the frame together. Then I biscuit, glue, and clamp the face frame to the cabinet.

## DOUBLE-STICK TAPE

I CAN'T REMEMBER WHERE I FIRST FOUND this type of double-stick tape, but life after double stick has certainly been a lot easier. I buy a ½-in.-wide Scotch®-brand product (www.3m.com) called Double Sided Tape. It's very thin, like one-sided Scotch tape, but it has great adhesion and is easy to peel off after I'm finished. I find it at stationery stores.

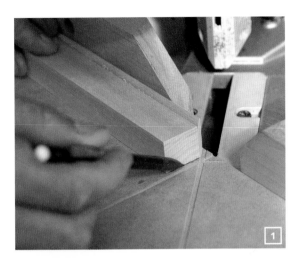
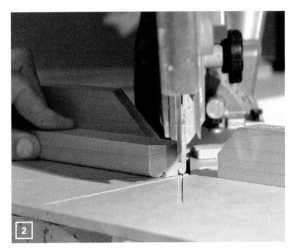

USE AN AUXILIARY TABLE TO JUDGE THE CUTS. I cut a piece of ¼ -in. MDF as an overlay on the miter-saw table, notched to wrap tightly around the fence so that there's no side-to-side play. I set the saw's depth of cut to just below the surface and make one 90-degree and two opposing 45-degree cuts. They serve as cut indicators; I can match the pencil line on the stock with the kerf and see exactly where the blade will go 1. When making two mitered cuts on the same piece, I rotate the stock and keep the saw in the same position so that the angle stays consistent 2.

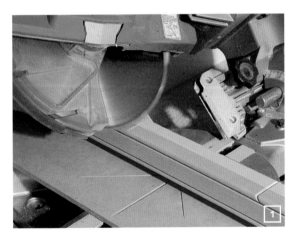

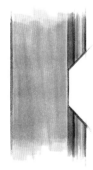

CUT MULTIPLES FOR ACCURATE ALIGNMENT. If two opposing pieces (the outer stiles, for example) share the same rail, I cut the miters at the same time for consistent results 1. I use double-stick tape to bind the two stiles together, then stand the pair on edge against the fence and miter the beads 2. Afterward, I pare down the waste to the shadowline with a sharp chisel 3.

# Installing Semicustom Cabinets

BY ISAAK MESTER

On the face of it, installing semicustom kitchen cabinets is pretty straightforward: Attach a run of boxes to the wall, make sure all the doors and drawers work, and don't scratch the paint. Unless kitchens are a regular part of your work week, however, you'll find that the installation can go sideways in a hurry if you don't pay attention to some key aspects of the job. In demonstrating the installation of this fairly typical kitchen, I illustrate the most important tricks of the trade that help to make this a professional-looking job.

## First, Unpack Carefully

The designer and the client picked semicustom cabinets from KraftMaid for the kitchen. In price and quality, they usually represent a comfortable midpoint between small-shop custom cabinets and big-box-store economy cabinets. The carcases are made of plywood, and the face frames, doors, and drawers are hardwood. The quality of the finishes is excellent. The cabinets were configured with a mix of drawer and door bases, two lazy-Susan corners, and some glass-door uppers. Cabinets like these are usually shipped to the job site. The first thing I do is check the shipping manifest against the items shipped and note any damaged or missing boxes.

**PROTECT THE FINISH.** Painter's tape on one edge of a level protects the cabinet finish. When the tape gets dirty, though, it's not helping any longer. Change it often.

The faster you start the return process, the faster you'll be able to finish the job.

When taking cabinets out of the boxes, use a knife only when necessary and don't cut the box along the cabinet's face or you may scratch the finish. Inspect each cabinet to make sure there are no dings, and arrange the return of any damaged units.

Factory cabinets are manufactured in part with hot-melt glue, which tends to dry in heavy drips that can get in the way of an installation. Before installing a cabinet, scrape off any of these drips.

Before installing a cabinet, remove its drawers and doors, set them aside, and replace them when the cabinet is set.

You'll need more shims than you think. An empty bucket keeps them handy and portable.

**START OFF ORGANIZED.** The best way to start an installation is to make sure that the space is clean and that your tools and materials are right where you need them. After unpacking the first run of cabinets, place them in the general vicinity of their future locations, leaving yourself enough space to work comfortably.

**WATCH THE KNIFE.** When opening the cabinet boxes with a knife, steer clear of the face of the cabinet. Don't get excited and learn this simple tip the hard way.

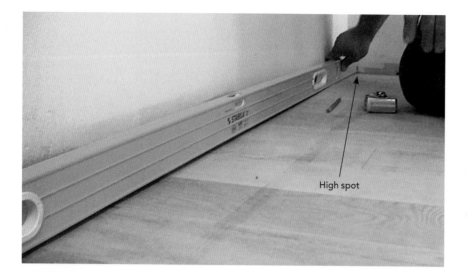

FIND THE HIGH SPOT.
Use a 6-ft. level to find
the highest point in the
floor, which becomes
the reference point to
set the cabinets. Extend
a level line outward to
determine how much
the adjacent cabinets
will have to be shimmed.
If the gap at the end of
the run is too large to
mask with trim, you'll
need to adjust (see the
facing page).

High spot

## Measure and Mark for Level

A level run of cabinets starts from a reference point
taken off the high spot on the floor or, when there
are soffits, the low spot on the ceiling. It's especially
important for the base cabinets to be level and flat
so that they can adequately support long runs of
countertop.

On this job, the kitchen's cathedral ceiling meant
that there were no constraints to the upper cabinets,
so we based our measurements on the floor. Using
a 6-ft. level, I checked the floor along the base of the
wall and found a high spot in the corner. Carried out
on a level line, this would translate to a gap of more
than an inch at the end of the cabinet run—too high
to hide with a kick plate or shoe molding.

To avoid this gap, I moved my reference point to
the end of the corner cabinet, where my original
level line cleared the floor by about $\frac{1}{2}$ in. I then
marked a new reference point $\frac{1}{4}$ in. below the original line. From this new point, I measured up
$34\frac{1}{2}$ in. to establish the height of the base cabinets
and drew a level line there. I then made another
mark $19\frac{1}{2}$ in. above that line to mark the bottom
of the upper cabinets, drawing that line out level
as well (see the photo on the facing page). When
installing the cabinets, I scribed and cut the bases
where the floor was higher than my reference mark,
and shimmed the bases where the floor was lower.

## Compensating for Corners

Once you've understood the state of the floor, you
have to scope out the walls. It's a rare event when
a kitchen's walls are plumb and square. I checked
to see that the corner itself was relatively square so
that the end cabinet on either side wouldn't flare out
from the wall. Corners are often less than square
because of the buildup of tape and compound.
Sometimes the best solution is to cut or scrape out
the compound behind the cabinet to square up the
corner.

I like to join the corner cabinet to the adjoining
cabinets before attaching them to the wall so that
I can carry the corner outward in two directions.
If the corner isn't square, I can adjust the cabinet's
angles so that there's an equal gap behind the end
cabinets, which I usually conceal with a finished end
panel. Here, because the line of cabinets was interrupted by appliances, I had the option of adjusting
the position of the cabinets independently, but I
always try to keep the counter overhang as consistent as possible.

There are times when joining your upper cabinets
together on the ground will make the installation
much easier and straighter. This is especially true
with frameless cabinets, as there is absolutely no
play in the installation. Some installers like to hang
the upper cabinets first because they don't have to

# ESTABLISH A REFERENCE LINE

Start a cabinet installation by finding the floor's high spot from which to create a level reference line on the wall to represent the cabinet tops. If the high spot is too high, split the difference. Mark a new reference point below the first line. Measure up 34½ in. to mark the top of the base cabinets.

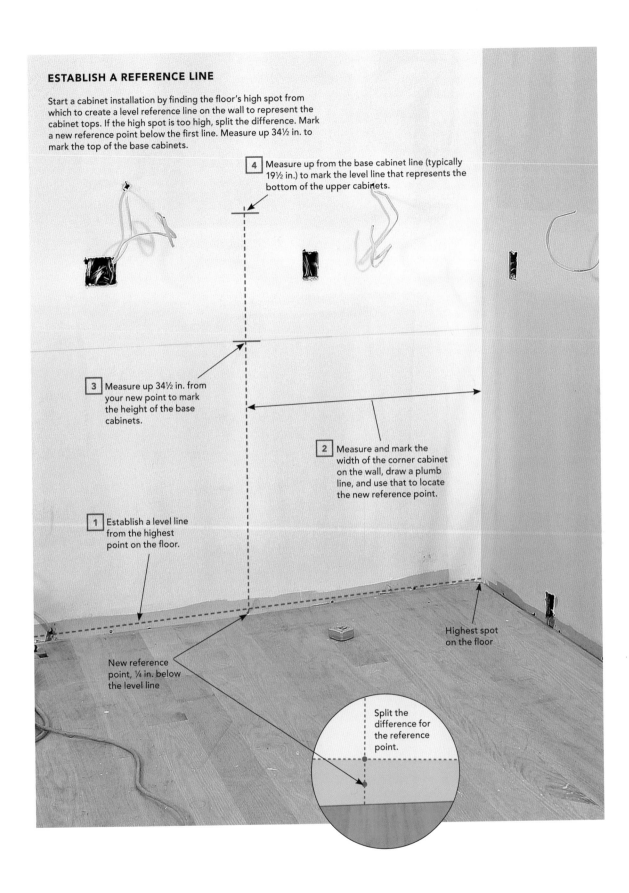

**4** Measure up from the base cabinet line (typically 19½ in.) to mark the level line that represents the bottom of the upper cabinets.

**3** Measure up 34½ in. from your new point to mark the height of the base cabinets.

**2** Measure and mark the width of the corner cabinet on the wall, draw a plumb line, and use that to locate the new reference point.

**1** Establish a level line from the highest point on the floor.

New reference point, ¼ in. below the level line

Highest spot on the floor

Split the difference for the reference point.

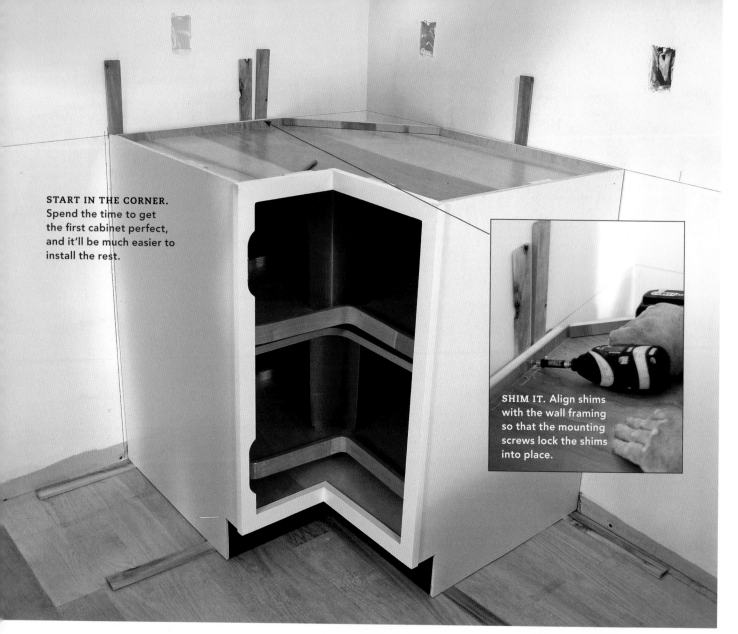

**START IN THE CORNER.** Spend the time to get the first cabinet perfect, and it'll be much easier to install the rest.

**SHIM IT.** Align shims with the wall framing so that the mounting screws lock the shims into place.

**GET IT RIGHT.** Many installations start in the corner, so that cabinet must be plumb, level, and square. Here, I had to cut down the corner cabinet to compensate for a high spot in the kitchen's inside corner. To make an accurate cut, I scribed the side panels ①, cut them down with a jigsaw ②, and transferred those cuts to the interior base supports ③. A couple of strategically placed shims brought the cabinet into level compliance.

When shimming the front of a cabinet, keep one finger on top of the face frame of the adjoining cabinet to avoid having to look to see when the two cabinets are even.

Dedicated drill-drivers—one for drilling pilot holes and one for driving screws—save time.

**SET CABINETS CAREFULLY.** As you work outward from the first cabinet, it's important to keep the successive cabinets level and in line with the walls.

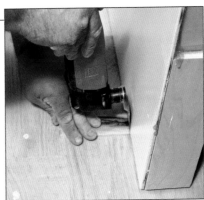

**TOOLS OF THE TRADE.** Use a small flat bar as a lever to gain more adjustment control when shimming a cabinet. A multitool does a clean and fast job of trimming shims without disturbing or splitting them.

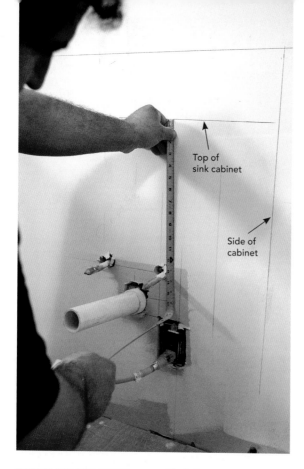

**ESTABLISH THE REFERENCE.** Find the centerline of the cabinet on the wall, then measure and mark the locations of the cabinet's side and top. Use only these two points to measure the plumbing and electrical locations.

**TRANSFER TO THE CABINET.** From the same two points, measure and mark the centers of the plumbing stubs and the outlet.

reach up and over the base cabinets. Many kitchen designs (like this one) are driven by appliance locations, though, so it's important to establish the base location first.

When it came to installing the upper cabinets, the first thing I did was to screw a length of scrap brick molding to the wall studs along the upper level line. This serves two purposes: First, it's a third hand to support the cabinets as they're installed; second, it makes a handy reference when locating screws inside the cabinet. If the area between the bases and the uppers isn't meant to be covered by a backsplash, it's easy enough to patch the screw holes in the walls.

## Keep Plumbing and Electrical Neat

One of the details that adds to a good installation is careful integration of cable and pipes in the cabinets. I have encountered too many kitchens where the

**DRILLING FOR APPEARANCES.** Drill ¼-in. pilot holes on the center marks from the cabinet back, then drill from the cabinet interior with a sharp hole saw, using its pilot bit as a guide, to minimize visible tearout.

**SET UPPER CABINETS WITH A LEDGER.** As with the lower cabinets, the upper-cabinet installation begins in the corner and works outward. Secondary support, such as a ledger or cabinet jack, helps to stabilize a cabinet's position while stud and wiring locations are marked and pilot holes drilled.

**START WITH A LEDGER.** Screw a temporary ledger such as a scrap piece of brick molding to studs in the wall to help support the upper cabinets. When screwing a cabinet to the wall, transfer the locations of the ledger screws to the inside of the cabinet.

**KEEP CABINETS IN LINE. (right)** Use padded bar clamps to attach the next cabinet in line with the first, making sure to align the face frames. Always countersink a pilot hole for screws, and use decking or similar heavy-duty screws to attach cabinets to each other and washer-head screws to attach cabinets to the wall. Drywall screws are too brittle and shouldn't be used.

**MOVE THE WIRES TO WHERE THEY BELONG.** Here, the undercabinet feeds should be above the cabinet bottom. On this job, a full backsplash will conceal the drywall repair.

**BACKING NOT INCLUDED.** Finished trim panels on the back of peninsulas often require extra nailing support. Layout lines on the walls help to locate blocking in the right places.

**KEEP FASTENERS CONCEALED.** Meant to be covered by corner trim or base, the perimeters are good spots to attach the panels and still keep the appearance clean.

installers simply hacked out a square in the cabinet back for the water and waste lines, which is visible whenever the cabinet is open. This not only looks messy, but it's also an easy entry point for pests.

The first step I take to ensure this integration is to insist that the plumber leave everything stubbed out and capped. It makes it easier to do a careful layout, which in turn makes a neater installation.

Second, I find out what kind of undercabinet lighting is going to be installed later so that I can drill the holes in the proper locations of the cabinets. There's nothing worse than seeing the lights installed with 2 ft. of exposed wire running

across the bottom of the cabinet to the hole that I drilled.

These may seem like small details, but it's the small details that signal a professional job.

## Scribing Shouldn't Be Difficult

Once the cabinets are in, the next step is to scribe and attach the finished end panels. Base moldings, often part of the trim package in semicustom cabinets, cover any gaps between the panels and the floor, so the wall is the critical area to be scribed. After measuring the space and determining the correct width or length of the panel, I shim or clamp

**THE EASIEST CROWN JOB.** Because of the cathedral ceiling in this kitchen, the cabinet crown could be cut simply by registering its spring angles onto the miter saw's table and fence.

**WORK CAREFULLY WITH PREFINISHED STOCK.** To reduce visible nail holes, it's a good idea to use the smallest nail or brad possible when attaching crown or other exposed trim.

the panel's top equal to the top of the cabinet. Setting a compass to the distance of the largest portion of the gap between the wall and the panel, I scribe the wall's line onto the panel, check the measurement to make sure it's right, and cut away the waste. Full-length panels should be shimmed plumb before they're scribed.

## Tips for Installing Trim

The trim for semicustom cabinets is usually made from prefinished hardwood, and it's relatively expensive and difficult to replace once you've started. Make sure you have enough before you sign off

on the delivery, although distributors often can send missing pieces within a few days. Because it's prefinished, the trim must be cut carefully to avoid tearout. Keep nail holes small so they can be concealed with a color-matched filler, and glue joints for extra holding power. When working with dark-stained crown, apply stain on the inside edges of miters so that any gaps won't show as prominently.

# Installing Kitchen Cabinets Smooth and Solo

BY MIKE GUERTIN

Installing kitchen cabinets is one of my favorite projects. Whether I'm working on a new home or on a remodeling project, cabinet installation signals that the end is in sight. And installing the right cabinets transforms an empty space into a functional, good-looking kitchen.

Even factory-made stock cabinets, though, can be fussy to install. Walls are rarely straight or floors flat. A two-person crew with basic tools requires at least a day to install an average-size kitchen. But thanks to a few specialty tools and some techniques I've developed through many years spent working alone, I can do the same work by myself.

Good planning and joining cabinets together prior to installation are two important strategies. Tools like a laser level, face-frame clamps, and a cabinet lift save time while also improving the accuracy of my work. Throughout the process, I do everything possible not to damage the new cabinets.

## Dings Don't Have to Happen

On most projects, a lot of work has gone into getting the kitchen ready for the cabinets. The cabinets are a finish item, and I take every precaution not to let them become damaged during installation, starting as soon as they are delivered. Even if the cabinets arrive on the job before I am ready for them, I unbox them immediately to make sure everything I ordered was delivered and to inspect them for damage. Before installing the cabinets, I number (on painter's tape) and remove the doors, shelves, and drawers to protect them from damage. Removing these parts also lightens the boxes and makes them easier to handle. I don't reinstall any parts until the rest of the kitchen is complete.

## Put the Plans on the Floor

For me, part of planning a smooth installation is drawing the cabinet layout as well as important plumbing and electrical information on the floor and walls. I draw the layout on the floor early in the construction process to help other tradesmen and myself proceed. This system speeds the installation process and helps me to avoid mistakes.

On the floor, I mark three lines parallel with the walls: the face of the wall cabinets, the face of the base cabinets, and the face of the rough toe kick. Then I mark the location of the individual base cabinets, wall cabinets, and appliances. I write the cabinet size code in each box and label the appliances and their sizes.

With all this information written on the floor, I can determine if I need filler strips and identify any potential conflicts, like an off-center range

outlet. The layout also shows the electrician and plumber where to locate rough-ins for appliances and fixtures. I also indicate on the floor and walls where pipe runs occur to avoid driving any cabinet-mounting screws into them.

## Accurate Elevations Help You to Get the Right Heights

On the walls, I mark stud, blocking, and utility locations as well as the top of the base cabinets and the bottom of the upper cabinets. I factor in the thickness of the finished flooring before these elevations are marked.

Stock base cabinets are 34½ in. tall (1½-in.-thick countertops bring the finished elevation of the base cabinets up to 36 in.). If you install the base cabinets on the subfloor and then cover the floor with ¾-in.-thick hardwood flooring, the countertop height will be short. So when I mark the elevation of the top of the base cabinets, I add the height of the finished flooring. In this case, I added ⅞ in. for a tile floor.

I always measure the elevation from the lowest spot I can find on the subfloor and use a laser level to mark the elevations at the ends of cabinet runs. Then I snap a chalkline or connect the points with a long spirit level. I also find the elevation of the bottom of the upper cabinets and use a stud finder to locate and mark the studs along both elevation lines.

When I install the base cabinets, I set them on plywood strips to shim them to the proper height. In fact, I cut plywood strips that are both thicker and thinner than I need and use them to make up for low and high spots in the subfloor. I cut the strips to equal the distance from the rough-toe-kick line

**MARK THE TOP OF THE BASE CABINETS AND THE BOTTOM OF THE UPPERS.** I use a laser level to mark the walls at the ends of each cabinet run. Then I snap chalklines to guide base- and upper-cabinet installation. Plan to shim the base cabinets off the subfloor the thickness of the finish flooring so that the 1½-in.-thick countertop will be 36 in. above the finish floor.

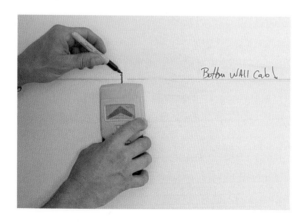

**FIND THE STUDS.** A stud finder locates framing members quickly. I indicate the stud locations with a tick mark along the chalklines. The marks still will be visible when the cabinets are in place.

# INSTALL BLOCKING TO ANCHOR CABINETS SOLIDLY

**YOU CAN FASTEN UPPER CABINETS** just to the studs, but horizontal blocking installed between the studs makes for a more secure installation. In new homes or gutted remodels, I install 2×4 or 2×6 blocks between studs. Make sure to locate blocking behind the cabinet's top mounting rail. When installing cabinets on existing walls (as shown here), I cut through the wallboard where the top mounting rail will land. I remove the wallboard and install 2×4 blocks with 3-in. screws. Then I cover the blocks with drywall and finish the seams with tape and compound.

to the wall (around 22 in.). And I set a strip at each end of a run of base cabinets and everywhere two cabinets meet. Later, when the base cabinets are installed, I use cedar shims to level and make fine adjustments to raise the tops of the cabinets to the chalkline.

## Upper or Base Cabinets First?

Professional kitchen installers debate whether the upper cabinets or the base cabinets should be mounted first. There's no right or wrong sequence, only preferences.

For many years, I installed the base cabinets first and laid boards over them to serve as a platform to rest the upper cabinets on during installation. But after damaging the face frames on a few base cabi-

nets with my belt buckle and tools dangling from my belt, I changed to mounting upper cabinets first and haven't looked back.

Before I install the upper cabinets I use a long spirit level, referencing the upper-cabinet positions marked on the floor, to draw plumb lines for the sides of the upper cabinets. This ensures that the upper cabinets will align with the base cabinets.

## Preassemble the Cabinets, and Forget about Wavy Walls

Walls are never flat. Even walls framed with engineered studs have bumps and dips at drywall seams. Sometimes cabinets aren't perfect, either. The side panels may be slightly out of square with the face frame, or a backing panel may not be flat

**USE CLAMPS TO DRAW THE STILES TOGETHER.** I use three screws in stiles 24 in. or taller and two screws in those shorter. Drill a ⅛-in.-dia. pilot hole through both stiles and a shallow ³⁄₁₆-in. hole into only the first stile to counterbore each trim-head screw. If possible, I locate the screws so that they'll be hidden by door hinges.

**FACE-FRAME CLAMPS.** Keeping the face frames of adjacent cabinets aligned while you screw them together is done easily with these special clamps (www.ponytools.com). The clamps have protective pads to keep new cabinets from being scratched and a drill guide to keep pilot holes straight. The guide flips out of the way, allowing you to drive the screw without removing the clamp.

**ALIGN THE CABINETS WITH A STRAIGHTEDGE.** Before joining the back of the cabinets, I put a straightedge across the top to make sure the tops are level and the front is straight. Then I shim between the side panels at the rear of the cabinet, and drive screws to keep the ganged cabinets straight. The cabinets now can be installed as a single unit.

across the rear. Imperfections in walls and cabinets make aligning the faces of cabinet runs difficult, particularly when cabinets are installed one at a time. I overcome these problems by ganging cabinets together before mounting them to the wall. This approach is faster and more precise than mounting cabinets individually.

Cabinets can be preassembled resting upright on the floor, on their backs, or elevated on a bench. I gang a run of cabinets together by screwing together the face-frame stiles and the rear of the cabinets. The trick is to clamp a straightedge along the top front of the cabinets while you screw them together. The front face and the top edge of the run need to be straight. Once the rear of the cabinets is joined, they will stay aligned.

I locate screws where they are least likely to be seen: Behind the hinges or in the drawer spaces on base cabinets. If a screw is needed where it can't be hidden, I countersink trim-head screws and cover them with color-matched filler. Screws joining the rear of the cabinets can be driven through the cabinet side panels above the top panel, where they'll never be noticed. I use three screws to join stiles taller than 24 in. and two screws in anything shorter. Two screws are plenty to hold the cabinet rears together. Once screwed together, the individual boxes essentially become one long cabinet.

When I install the cabinet run as a unit, I still have to check the whole run for level using both a spirit level and the elevation lines. I make adjustments once for the whole run of cabinets instead of making many adjustments for each individual cabinet. I usually can move long runs of base cabinets into place by myself, but sometimes I need help with upper cabinets.

## Wall Cabinets Get a Lift

Two people easily can lift a gang of three to six wall cabinets when the doors and shelves have been removed. But I work alone a lot, so I rely on a cabinet lift. For me, the cabinet lift has been worth every penny I spent on it, but if you're doing one kitchen-

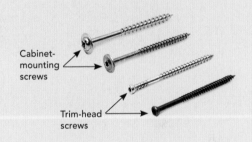
cabinet installation, you usually can find a lift at a rental center. The lift's table supports up to 6 ft. of ganged cabinets. For longer cabinet gangs, I screw a plank to the lift's table.

I roll the cabinets to the wall while they are still low on the lift, then crank them up. This keeps the center of gravity down and makes the lift less likely to tip. When I'm 3 in. from the wall, I raise the cabinets up to the mounting line, mark and drill pilot holes for mounting screws, and cut openings for utilities and undercabinet-lighting wires.

A cabinet lift isn't necessary to mount wall cabinets; it just makes the job easier. For short runs of

# SMOOTH MOVE: PREINSTALLED CROWN MOLDING

I THINK IT'S EASIER TO APPLY CROWN MOLDING to the cabinets with the preassembled unit on the floor. To do this, however, I first have to lift the cabinets into position and mark the bottom of the crown on each end of the bank of cabinets and at all cabinet joints. I then can lower the cabinets, screw blocking to the top rails, and install the crown by screwing through the blocking and into the crown from behind. With this technique, there are no nail holes that need to be filled with color-matched putty.

CABINET LIFT. Hanging a run of upper cabinets by yourself isn't a problem if you use a cabinet lift (www.e-zspreadnlift .com). Available at rental centers, this tool also can be used to roll base cabinets into position.

HANGING CABINETS WITH A LEDGER IN-STEAD OF A LIFT. If you don't have a cabinet lift, you can screw a temporary ledger board along the chalkline to support the back of a wall unit and wedge a wood prop in place to support the front while you drive installation screws. But I prefer to have a helper, especially for longer runs of cabinets.

cabinets, you can screw a temporary 1×3 ledger to the wall to support the cabinets. If you use a ledger, drill pilot holes and twist screws into the holes at both ends of the cabinet run before lifting it to the wall. The ledger will help as you balance the cabinets with one hand and drive the screw with the other. Long gangs of cabinets can be lifted onto a ledger by two people. One person can hold the top against the wall while the other drives the screws.

I also preassemble the base cabinets. After shimming the ganged base cabinets to the appropriate elevation, I fasten them to the wall at each stud, using shims to fill any hollows.

Installing doors and drawers is the last thing I do on a project. I wait until the countertops are set, the plumbing is connected, everything is painted, and the flooring is installed. Waiting until the end of the project protects the cabinet doors and drawer fronts from collateral damage as the project is completed.

**DRILL HOLES FOR WIRING.**
With the lift holding the cabinet close to the wall, I can drill holes to wire undercabinet lights exactly where they need to be.

**DRIVE SCREWS INTO STUDS AND BLOCKING.** Cabinet-installation screws require pilot holes. I drive screws into the studs above the top panel of the cabinet, below the bottom panel, or through the back. When blocking is installed (see p. 93), I drill holes 2 in. from the side panels through the mounting rail and about 12 in. apart. With the unit secured to the wall with at least four screws, I remove the lift and drive the remaining screws.

**PREASSEMBLED UPPER CABINETS HANG AS ONE UNIT.** Cabinets make the lift top heavy, so I roll the lift close to the wall before cranking the ganged cabinets up and positioning them against their layout lines. Don't risk dropping the cabinets; clamp them to the lift's table until they are screwed to the wall.

**KEEP THE TOPS FLUSH AND THE FRONT STRAIGHT.** Join the base cabinets together with trim screws through the stiles. Shim between and screw together the panels in the back. Use a straightedge across the front of ganged base cabinets to keep the tops flush and the fronts straight. If the cabinets are imperfect, I sometimes have to plane the tops down to get surfaces flush.

**USE A GAUGE STICK TO PAD OUT THE FLOOR.** Due to the fluctuations in the subfloor, the plywood strips won't all be the same thickness. I rip 2-in.-wide strips of ¼-in., ½-in., and ¾-in. plywood and use a 34 ¼-in. gauge stick (the height of the cabinets less the countertop) to determine which size strip to use. I place strips at each end of a run of cabinets and anywhere cabinets are joined.

**SHIM FOR WAVY WALLS.** (above) I drill pilot holes at each stud location and drive screws to secure the cabinets. Shims fill the hollows between the mounting rails and walls.

**SET BASE CABINETS ON THE STRIPS, THEN SHIM.** (left) After setting a gang of base cabinets into position on the plywood strips, I use shims to make sure they are sturdy and level.

# CORNER DETAILS

## BETTER SUPPORT FOR SINGLE CABINETS

Cabinets less than 24 in. wide that stand alone or next to an appliance are prone to movement. I secure the bottom front on these cabinets by mounting a 2× block to the floor just inside the rough toe kick. I drop the cabinet over the blocking and screw through the rough toe kick.

## A FACE FRAME TAKES THE PLACE
## OF A CORNER CABINET

Angled base cabinets for inside-corner sinks are expensive. Rather than buy an unnecessary box, I order an extra face-frame panel and a door from the cabinet company and use them to connect the base cabinets on both sides of the sink. The side panels of the adjoining cabinets and the painted drywall become the inside walls of the cabinet. I mount blocking to the sides of the adjacent cabinets and along the walls to support a plywood bottom panel with holes drilled for the plumbing. To support the countertop, I screw cleats to the walls. If the inside-corner cabinet will house a sink, I leave it open. If it is for storage, I make it a lazy Susan.

# How to Install Inset Cabinet Doors

BY SCOTT GIBSON

Making and fitting cabinet doors takes time, and it has its occasional frustrations. Still, installing doors correctly is one of the real pleasures of cabinetmaking. If everything isn't flat and square or if the hinges aren't installed properly, the doors won't work the way they should. For an overlay cabinet door, the process is more forgiving: The door simply closes against the cabinet or face frame. An inset door is another story. It has to be trimmed to fit the door opening exactly, with an even gap all around between the face frame and the door.

I like the appearance of inset doors because they don't look as clunky as overlay doors. When an inset door is fitted correctly with a narrow, even reveal, the cabinet has a line of detail that is otherwise missing. This more finished look is associated both with traditional designs, such as Shaker, and with more modern styles. A cabinet built with inset doors also says something about the cabinetmaker. Although making inset cabinet doors takes time, the results are worth it to me, and the process goes surprisingly quickly once you've honed the technique.

For this kitchen project, I built the carcases first, then added the face frames. Typically, I use butt hinges (more on that later), so I mark and cut the hinge mortises on the face frames before I attach them to the carcases. I like to cut the hinge mortises

on the stiles before the face frames are even glued up. I just pop a piece in the vise, cut the mortises, and I'm done.

The doors are next. I start by building a door to the same dimensions as the opening. It's tempting to make it slightly smaller so that there's less trimming involved, but that move can backfire. When gluing up the door, make every effort to keep it flat. You can compensate for a slight amount of twist (see "In a Perfect World, Doors Are Flat," on p. 107), but if the door is too badly skewed, you'll have to make another one. If the door or the opening is out of square,

## TOOL TALK

**THE LIE-NIELSEN® LOW-ANGLE JACK PLANE** that I use has a thick plane iron that's set at 12 degrees, which slices easily through difficult end grain. It's pricey, but it's the kind of tool that makes the work much easier. I'm always dragging it out onto my bench.

**DECIDE ON THE SIZE OF THE REVEAL.** On a tablesaw, cut a shim equal in thickness to the reveal (⅛ in. on a side is typical for paint-grade work), and trim it to length so that it can sit inside the bottom of the door opening.

**BEGIN TO TRIM THE DOOR.** Use a low-angle jack plane to flatten the bottom of the door. Because the stile's end grain is exposed at the door's top and bottom, work inward from each edge to avoid tearout. Another method is to use a crosscut sled on a tablesaw and, referencing the door's hinge side against the fence, trim the bottom of the door.

fitting the door may result in a reveal that looks too big. Ideally, the door opening and the door itself will be square, but that's often not the case. Once the cabinet and the door are made, forget about square and deal with what's there.

I trim one edge of the door at a time and then work my way around, beginning with the bottom of the door and ending at the strike-side stile. It's possible to do all of this work with hand tools alone, but it's faster and sometimes more accurate to do at least some of the cutting on a tablesaw and, if you have access to one, a jointer. The tool choice is yours.

When I've fitted the door, I place it in the opening and mark the hinge locations. I like to use good-quality brass butt hinges. To me, butt hinges look best on traditional cabinets. I see that classic hinge barrel paired with an even reveal and think, "That looks right." While I appreciate that European hinges are easy to adjust to get a door to hang properly, I have never gotten past how big and bulky they look when you open the door. I've also used some European hinges that will not hold their adjustment. Surface-mounted hinges look fine on some styles of cabinets, but I never seem to build anything in those styles. Piano hinges are great for heavy, specialty doors, but they're not an everyday item. Ditto for concealed hinges. If I were building cabinets that have really contemporary, minimalist styles, I think that my choices might be somewhat different.

HINGE SIDE IS NEXT TO BE FITTED.

BOTTOM SHIM CREATES A REFERENCE.

**DON'T CARE ABOUT SQUARE.** The idea is to fit the door in the opening, not make a square door. With the door in the opening atop the shim, press the hinge side against the stile. Ideally, there should be a consistently tight fit from top to bottom on that side. This gets a little awkward because the door won't go completely into the opening quite yet. (Just try not to drop the door, as the author did.)

**ADJUST BY SHAVING.** If necessary, use a jointer or similar plane to adjust the door's hinge side until it fits tightly against the face-frame stile while resting on the bottom shim.

# USE A BOARD JACK

It's difficult to secure a cabinet door in a bench vise so that the work is well supported and at a convenient height. The author made this support (historically called a board jack) from plywood scraps. He attached an appropriately sized leg to a block screwed to the benchtop, then reinforced the leg with a plywood gusset. For this job, he made one jack for working vertically and another for working horizontally.

DON'T REMOVE TOO MUCH MATERIAL. The top is trimmed in two steps to minimize the risk of taking off too much of the door. Begin by placing the door on the bottom shim and marking both sides of the top of the door so that it will fit just inside the opening (top left and above). Trim off the excess on the tablesaw with a crosscut sled (left). Remember to reference the hinge side against the fence. If the amount to be removed isn't a 90-degree cut, insert shims between the sled fence and the door edge to adjust the angle of the cut. Check the fit, and then mark the reveal at both sides so that it equals the reveal at the bottom. Trim the reveal to the marks with the crosscut sled, using the same shims if necessary.

GO FOR THE TIGHT FIT FIRST. It's best to cut the hinge mortises on the face frame before it's assembled. If you haven't done so though, now's the time. Mark and trim the strike edge of the door, either with a pass on the tablesaw or with a handplane. The door should squeeze into the opening so that there will be just enough space to install hinges. With the bottom of the door still resting on the shim, mark the hinge locations on the door (above).

# TOOL TALK

ONE OF MY FAVORITE TOOLS in my shop is a simple knife made from a short length of an old file. The handle isn't fancy, but the blade is superb. My dad gave me the knife when I first started making furniture. Now that he's gone, it's pretty special. Because it has a double bevel, it's not as good as a marking knife, but it has many other uses.

Possibly my most important tool for projects such as cabinet doors is my Lie-Nielsen low-angle block plane. A standard block plane's blade is mounted at a 20-degree angle to the sole. A low-angle's blade is mounted at 12 degrees, which makes it possible to plane end grain and cross-grain without tearout. It's great for removing millmarks, adjusting the fit of a drawer or door, truing up mortise-and-tenon joints, and a hundred other things. Lie-Nielsen uses excellent steel that takes a good edge and stays sharp for a long time. The body is bronze and doesn't rust. I've had this plane for a long time and have dropped it on concrete floors more than once, so it's a little dinged. Still, it works beautifully. My son made the leather case for it.

CUT THE MORTISES. Move the door into a bench vise and mark the mortise locations with a chisel. With a carbide straight spiral bit chucked into a laminate trimmer, use the hinge plate as a gauge to set the depth of the bit and cut the mortises (above). A piece of ¾-in. scrap clamped to the back side of the door creates a more stable base for the trimmer (left).

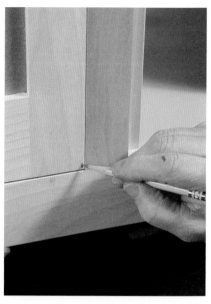

**KEEP YOUR OPTIONS OPEN.** Remove the shim, hang the door with only one screw per hinge leaf, and check the fit. The strike side will probably need an adjustment or a back bevel. If not, and if the door closes evenly against the stop, put in the rest of the hinge screws.

## The Correct Reveal Is Consistent and Not Too Thin

After you've built and installed a few doors, it's easy to see where the pitfalls lie. For the most part, it's all about the reveal. It's tempting to make a very narrow reveal (1/16 in. or less) because it looks so classy when it's done. Tolerances this small, though, lead to trouble. In the summer, even frame-and-panel doors swell slightly; at any time of year, the wood can twist or warp slightly, causing the doors to bind. This is much harder to judge on painted doors because you have to take into account the thickness of the paint when you fit them. Going back to refit a door that's painted is a nuisance.

Doors that are too loose look like the builder didn't care enough to get it right. An uneven reveal is worse because your eye instantly picks up on it. It's obviously out of level or plumb, like a crooked picture frame on a wall. I think the best compromise is to err a little on the loose side and make the reveal even.

# IN A PERFECT WORLD, DOORS ARE FLAT

**THEORETICALLY, ALL DOORS AND FACE FRAMES** are square and flat; in reality, they're often not. A door that's slightly twisted might hit the strike with one corner before the other and not close properly (see the photos below).

There's no perfect solution to this problem, but you can try adjusting the position of the hinges on either the door or the cabinet to compensate. Take out the single screw you've used, move the hinge in or out, and insert a screw through another hole to fix the hinge in its new position. You can glue a sliver of wood into the first hole and redrill it later.

It may take more than one try and adjustments in both hinges before you find the best compromise. You want the door to close evenly on the stop; a tiny lip at one corner of the opening won't be noticeable.

If you can't get all the way there by adjusting the hinge positions, plane the back side of the door where it first strikes the stop. Reducing the thickness of the door by a few passes of a plane shouldn't be visible to the casual eye.

**WHEN A DOOR GOES WRONG.** A warped door won't land evenly on the strike side and may protrude beyond the face frame at the top or bottom.

**SHIFT ONE HINGE.** By moving the location of the hinge diagonally opposite the problem corner (left), it's possible to make the door land evenly on the strike. Mark the leaf location before moving it.

**REDUCE THE DOOR.** The alternative is to plane the back side of the door where it hits the strike (right) until the entire side hits evenly.

# Crown Molding for Kitchen Cabinets

BY GARY STRIEGLER

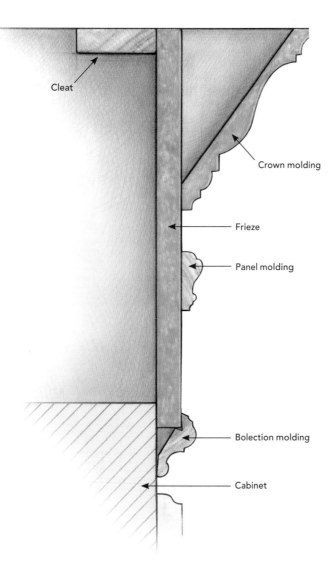

Cleat

Crown molding

Frieze

Panel molding

Bolection molding

Cabinet

When I started building, ceilings were 8 ft. tall. In the kitchen, a clunky soffit dropped down a foot above the cabinets, limiting them to 7 ft. in height. When ceiling heights grew to 9 ft., kitchen cabinets grew another foot or so to about 8 ft. Who couldn't use the extra storage? But that was the limit for kitchen cabinets, because close to no one can reach higher than that without a ladder. Still, in my market, ceiling height continued to grow to about 10 ft. What do you do with the space above the cabinets? One solution is to leave it open as display space. Of course, that adds costs for lighting and display items, never mind the extra dusting.

In response, some of my clients asked about taking their upper cabinets all the way to the ceiling, which at least minimizes the dusting. But just growing the upper cabinets by 2 ft. would put the proportions way out of balance. Plus, manufacturers don't want to warrant a door that tall. One solution was to add a set of short cabinets with glass doors. That cuts way back on the dusting, and the extra row of cabinets looks great. However, it can add several thousand dollars to the cabinet budget. I needed a third option that would be less expensive than adding cabinets and involve less maintenance than open tops. The

**TWO POINTS MAKE A LINE.** Use a level to plumb up from the face of the cabinet and to establish the endpoints of the cleat.

solution turned out to be adding a decorative frieze above standard wall cabinets.

The whole assembly is relatively inexpensive to build, consisting merely of a flat frieze board that supports crown, panel, and bolection molding. It looks great, ties into the kitchen crown molding, and needs little dusting. It took my lead carpenter and me a bit over a day to build the frieze for the kitchen shown here. Kitchens vary, of course: Ceiling height, cabinet height, style, and finishes will affect your final design. Because this custom kitchen was later painted on site, the frieze ended up blending seamlessly with both the room and the cabinets. If you use prefinished cabinets, you can get finished plywood and moldings from most manufacturers that can be used in the same way.

## Cleats Outline the Frieze

I fasten the top of the frieze to cleats nailed to the ceiling and plumb with the face of the cabinets. To ensure that the top of long runs of frieze will be straight, I establish two endpoints and snap a chalkline on the ceiling. I make the cleats from scraps of whatever the frieze-board material is—in this case, ¾-in. MDF. The material doesn't matter as much as making sure it's straight so that any irregularities don't telegraph to the face of the frieze.

**NAIL THE CLEAT TO THE CEILING.** If the cleat crosses joists, nail to them. If not, spread glue on the back of the cleat and secure it while the glue sets by driving nails at opposing angles into the drywall.

## Frieze Board Is the Foundation

Because this kitchen was going to be painted, my lead carpenter and I ripped the frieze board from ¾-in. MDF shelf board. MDF is stable and holds paint well, and shelf board is a convenient way to buy it. We mitered the outside corners and butted the insides. The inside and outside corners had to look good, but the fit against the ceiling and the tops of the cabinets didn't matter much because we were adding moldings in both places.

**REINFORCING A CORNER.** When there are no joists at a corner, reinforce the cleats by adding a second layer.

## ADD A NAILER FOR THE CROWN

WHEN THE JOISTS RUN perpendicular to the cabinets, they provide nailing every 16 in. When they don't, a piece of 2× stock glued to the drywall offers a solid attachment for crown. Once it dries, carpenter's glue does a surprisingly good job of holding the nailer in place. The trick is securing the piece until the glue dries. For that, drive in long finish nails at opposing angles.

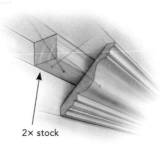

2× stock

MARK THE CABINET. Because they're so close, any variation in spacing between the frieze board and the tops of the doors would be obvious. Mark the frieze location carefully.

NAIL THE FRIEZE BOARD. Be sure to hit both the tops of the cabinets and the cleats on the ceiling.

CHECK FOR PLUMB. To ensure tight joints, it's crucial that the frieze be plumb. Sometimes a shim or two is required.

NOTCH, AND ADD NAILERS AS NEEDED. Some pieces of frieze board will extend behind others. Notches allow them to clear the cabinets and the cleats. Nailers provide attachment for the abutting frieze board.

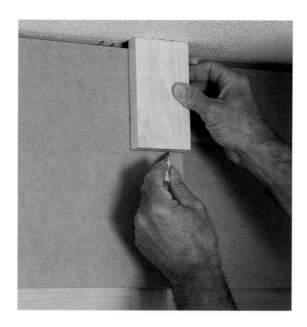

**MARK THE CROWN'S BOTTOM.** Use a block cut to the length of the crown's drop to mark the location of the crown's bottom on the frieze.

**MARK THE CROWN'S TOP.** To locate the top, hold a scrap of crown to the bottom line.

## Mark the Crown's Location

When installing crown molding for cabinets, the lengths are typically short, so I like to mark the crown for cutting by holding it in place. To ensure I'm holding it at a consistent angle, I mark the location of the crown's top on the ceiling and its bottom on the frieze board. I determine the crown's drop from the ceiling by holding a scrap inside a square and noting the measurement, which I use to make a gauge block.

## Cutting Crown Miters on the Flat

Wider crown, such as the 7-in. material used here, can't be cut standing up on most miter saws, so it has to be cut lying flat. If the crown is the most common configuration, which springs off the wall at 38 degrees and meets the ceiling at 52 degrees, set the saw at a 33.9-degree bevel and a 31.6-degree miter. Most compound-miter saws have marks or detents at these locations. Many newer saws bevel to the left and the right, but older saws as well as some new ones bevel to one side only, usually with the saw tilting to the left, as shown on the facing page.

## Tackle Tough Pieces First

I start with the most difficult sections, which are typically the short ones, or where there's a piece with two inside corners. Sections with short runs are easier to assemble on a bench; that way, you're sure to get a tight fit. I cut one end of the longer sections, then hold the pieces in place to check the fit before marking the other end for cutting.

**THE MOST COMMON CROWN CONFIGURATION**

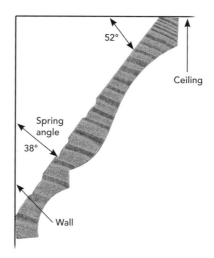

52°

Ceiling

Spring angle

38°

Wall

# CUTTING CROWN MITERS

**SET THE MITER ANGLE TO THE LEFT**

To cut the left half of an outside corner or the right half of an inside corner, set the miter 31.6 degrees to the left and position the bottom of the crown against the fence.

**Outside corner**

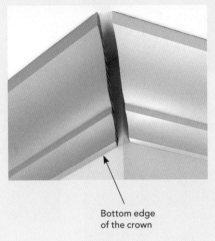

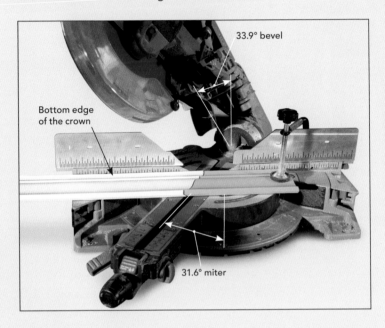

33.9° bevel

Bottom edge of the crown

31.6° miter

Bottom edge of the crown

**SET THE MITER ANGLE TO THE RIGHT**

To cut the left half of an inside corner or the right half of an outside corner, set the miter 31.6 degrees to the right and position the top of the crown against the fence.

**Inside corner**

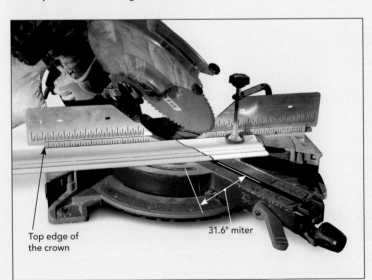

Top edge of the crown

31.6° miter

**ASSEMBLE SHORT SECTIONS.** Use glue and brad nails to join short sections to longer pieces prior to installation.

**NAILING IN PLACE.** Holding the crown on the lines, fasten it to the frieze and ceiling.

**FASTEN THE JOINT.** Spread some glue inside the joint, and reinforce it with brads.

## Bolection Molding Adds Interest

I had options for the panel molding below the frieze board, but I selected a bolection molding. Most panel moldings (also known as base cap) are ¾ in. thick and would just butt up to the frieze. Bolection molding is milled so that the top edge of the molding lips over the piece above, hiding the joint as well as adding depth and interest. When being cut, bolection molding has to be held at the angle it will be installed.

## Panel Molding Breaks Up a Wide Board

Adding a panel mold below the crown breaks up the wide frieze and adds interest. I find that placing the band of panel molding about two-thirds of the way between the crown and the bolection is about the right proportion. Unlike the crown and the bolection, panel molding is simply cut flat against the fence.

**ADD A SACRIFICIAL SHIM UNDER THE BOLECTION WHEN CUTTING.** To get the correct angle, make the shim the same thickness as the piece the molding lips over.

**NAIL THE BOLECTION HOME.** Hold the lip of the bolection molding tight to the edge of the frieze when nailing.

**LOCATE THE BOTTOM OF THE PANEL MOLDING.** Holding a block against the crown ensures a consistent line.

**NAIL THE PANEL MOLDING ALONG THE LAYOUT LINES.** (above) Particularly with longer pieces, installing along the lines straightens any warped molding.

**MARKING IN PLACE MAKES FOR ACCURATE CUTS.** (left) Make sure the first end of the piece fits well, then mark the second end with a sharp pencil.

# Vanities and Other Standalone Cabinets

# Build a Floating Vanity

BY NANCY R. HILLER

As someone who prefers not to be vexed by job-related anxieties in the wee hours, I work hard to prevent foreseeable problems. On most jobs, gravity is the cabinetmaker's friend. When it comes to floating furniture, however, gravity poses certain challenges. If you don't take these challenges seriously, you may find yourself with a cabinet that wants to fall apart—or worse, one that falls off the wall.

*Fine Homebuilding* asked me to build a bathroom vanity for their Project House, and structural challenges were only one of the issues. Designed by architect Duncan McPherson, the cabinet's sleek, clean look depended on careful planning and on maintaining sharp lines. The vanity also was intended to be compliant with the Americans with Disabilities Act, so the center portion below the sink was to be removable for wheelchair access.

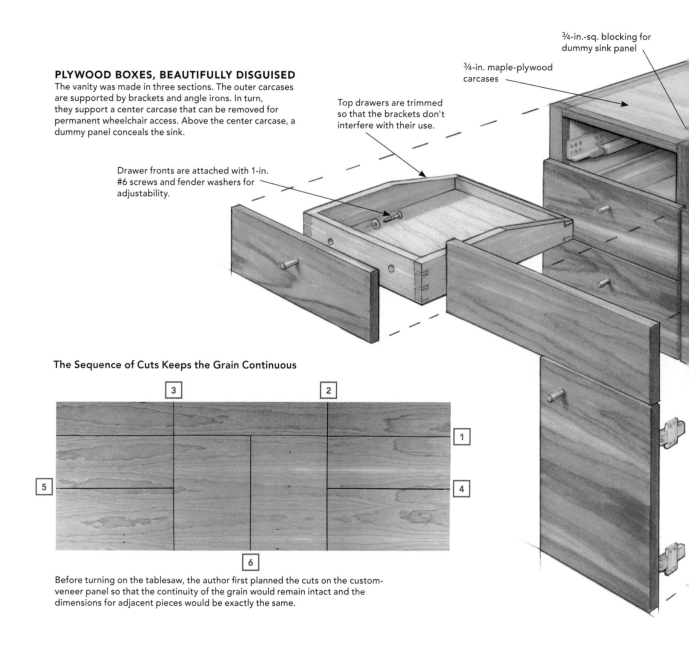

**PLYWOOD BOXES, BEAUTIFULLY DISGUISED**

The vanity was made in three sections. The outer carcases are supported by brackets and angle irons. In turn, they support a center carcase that can be removed for permanent wheelchair access. Above the center carcase, a dummy panel conceals the sink.

¾-in.-sq. blocking for dummy sink panel

¾-in. maple-plywood carcases

Top drawers are trimmed so that the brackets don't interfere with their use.

Drawer fronts are attached with 1-in. #6 screws and fender washers for adjustability.

**The Sequence of Cuts Keeps the Grain Continuous**

3   2

1

5   4

6

Before turning on the tablesaw, the author first planned the cuts on the custom-veneer panel so that the continuity of the grain would remain intact and the dimensions for adjacent pieces would be exactly the same.

To accentuate the horizontal shape, I wanted to wrap the exterior in the continuous grain of cherry-veneered moisture-resistant MDF; the carcases could be made from maple plywood. Solid maple drawers would be dovetailed for looks and strength.

## Strength from Fasteners and Face Frames

To build the cabinets, I began by cutting the case parts from prefinished ¾-in.-thick maple plywood. Because the sides of this cabinet were to have

finished panels applied during installation, the ¼-in. plywood backs could simply be applied to the back of the cases, instead of housed in a groove or a rabbet.

To ensure the strength of these cabinets, I built them with biscuits interspersed with 2-in. Confirmat screws. After gluing and clamping the cases, I cleaned up glue squeeze-out and installed the screws.

Although the design is European-inspired, I added face frames to reinforce the structure of the cases and to have an alternative to veneer tape for covering the plywood edges.

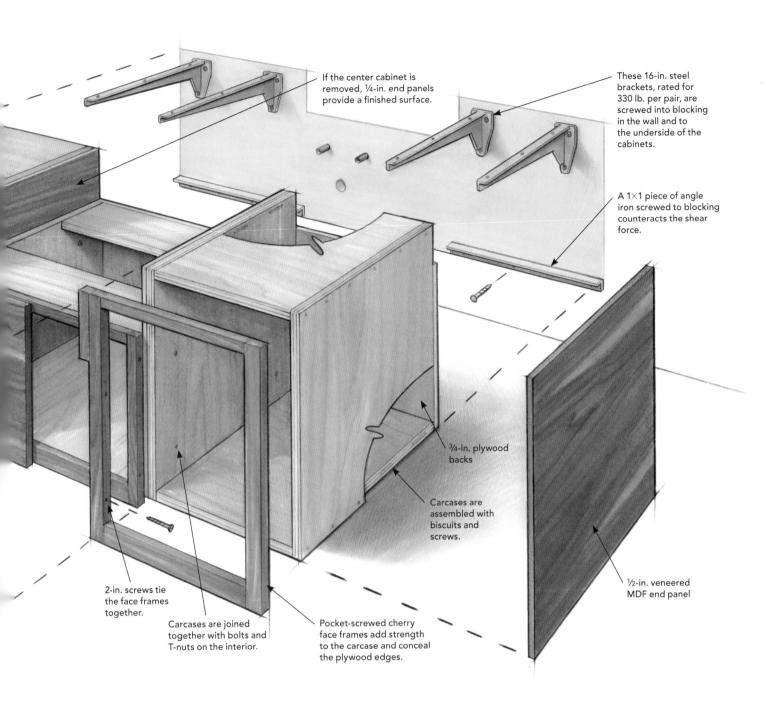

If the center cabinet is removed, ¼-in. end panels provide a finished surface.

These 16-in. steel brackets, rated for 330 lb. per pair, are screwed into blocking in the wall and to the underside of the cabinets.

A 1×1 piece of angle iron screwed to blocking counteracts the shear force.

¾-in. plywood backs

Carcases are assembled with biscuits and screws.

½-in. veneered MDF end panel

2-in. screws tie the face frames together.

Carcases are joined together with bolts and T-nuts on the interior.

Pocket-screwed cherry face frames add strength to the carcase and conceal the plywood edges.

I milled solid-cherry stiles and rails and joined the parts with pocket screws to make the face frames. I attached each frame to its case with glue and clamps, positioning the clamps inside the box so that pressure would be applied at the visible joints between case edge and face frame. After cutting the ¼-in. backs for all three cases, I test-fit the cases to each other in their final configuration, using T-nuts, bolts, and screws to attach the removable center case to the outer sections.

## Dovetailed Drawers Are Easy with the Right Jig

Once the cases were fitted with their face frames, I installed the drawer slides. This way I knew the exact dimensions of the drawer boxes. I also kept the hardware in mind when determining where to cut the grooves for drawer bottoms, because some types of drawer slides require a specific location relative to the bottom of the drawer side.

After cutting out the drawer parts from solid maple, I sanded the interior faces and set up the dovetail jig.

START WITH STRONG BOXES. Because the cabinets were fairly deep and cantilevered from the wall, the carcases had to be built to resist racking. The author first used biscuits to connect butt-jointed sides. Then she drilled pilot holes between the biscuits with a stepped bit and added beefy Confirmat screws (right).

CLAMPING UP SQUARE. At this point in the assembly, the carcases don't have backs or anything else that will keep the four sides square until the glue dries. As I clamp together each carcase, I measure the diagonals (above left). If the diagonals aren't equal, I offset the clamps on one side (above right) until the box is square.

Dovetails make a strong, beautiful drawer, but there was no reason for me to cut them by hand. Using a Keller jig (see the sidebar on the facing page), I can cut the four parts for one drawer in about 10 minutes. I cut the grooves for the ¼-in. plywood bottoms on the tablesaw and ripped the drawer backs at the grooves so that I could insert the bottoms into the grooves after the sides were assembled. Once the drawers were glued and clamped, I made sure that they were square and flat. I sanded the drawer boxes when the glue was dry, then inserted the drawer bottoms and fixed them each in place with two small screws.

WHEN I'M MAKING CABINETS I'm in a production mindset, so I use a router and a jig to cut the drawer dovetails. I've used several jigs, but the Keller jig is my favorite. It's incredibly simple and efficient, and it produces beautiful joints. The jig consists of two aluminum templates, one for the pins and one for the tails, which are clamped to the respective pieces. The set comes with top bearing-guided router bits.

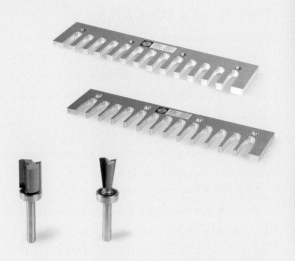

## Doors and Drawer Fronts from Custom-Veneer Material

I could have bought a sheet of ¾-in. cherry plywood off the shelf to create the vanity front, but including the end panels meant that I'd need more than one sheet, and then the grain wouldn't be continuous. Luckily, there's a custom-veneer place in town where I was able to choose the veneer and how it would be laid up on three separate panels (see the sidebar on p. 122).

**BOTTOM SLIDES IN LAST.** After the glue had dried and the drawer assembly was square and flat, the author slid the plywood bottom into its groove and fastened it with small screws to the underside of the back.

## CUSTOM VENEER IS A GAME CHANGER

I CONSIDER MYSELF LUCKY to live in Bloomington, because there's a world-class custom-veneer shop right in town. Although Heitink Architectural Veneer and Plywood supplies more than 120 species of veneered products to architectural millwork clients for enormous commercial projects (Las Vegas casinos, for example), it also makes small projects like this one possible. Pallets of veneer come into the factory and are trimmed, glued, and spliced into sheets. The sheets then are laminated to substrates of any size or type. Heitink can arrange the panels' grain patterns to match sequentially so that an entire room can be wrapped in a unique pattern of wood grain.

**NOTHING GETS BY THE INSPECTOR.** After the veneer sheets are glued up, each is checked on a big light table for cracks, imperfections, and other hidden defects.

I marked out the door and drawer faces on the plywood so that the grain alignment would be continuous across the face of the cabinet. I cut the drawer fronts and doors, then edge-banded them with heat-sensitive veneer tape and sanded the tape flush at the edges. I also drilled holes and mounted the European hinges on the doors. After locating the hinge plates on the inside faces of the center cabinet by holding the doors in position and placing marks directly on the inside of the case, I put the doors aside until the cabinet installation.

## Finish for a Wet Area

Bathroom cabinets should have a water-resistant finish. If I were building more cabinets, I would have them sprayed with a conversion varnish; for this one cabinet, though, I brushed on several coats of oil-based polyurethane. To prepare the cabinet parts for the polyurethane, I vacuumed, then wiped it all down with a tack rag moistened with mineral spirits to remove any remaining dust.

After brushing on a coat of polyurethane, I let it dry thoroughly overnight. The next day, I scuffed up the surfaces with 220-grit sandpaper, tacked again, and applied a second coat. I repeated the whole thing for a third coat, too.

## Putting It in Place

Once on site, I began the installation by placing 2× blocking between the studs in the wall. Usually you have to remove drywall to access the stud bays, but if you're careful you can hide repairs behind the cabinet. (On this project I had access to the back of the tiled wall.) Using heavy construction screws, I attached one line of blocking to support brackets for the top of the cabinet and another line below for angle iron at the base.

Next, I found the centerline of the wall and marked a horizontal line for the top of the casework. I located the tops of the upper brackets by measuring down ¾ in. from the line. Each outside cabinet would be supported by two brackets positioned as close as possible toward the sides of each case to

**DIAL IN A PRECISE FIT.** To scribe each end panel to the wall, the author clamped the panel flush to the outside of the ¾-in. face frame, then used a ¾-in. scrap to mark the wall's contour.

**MEASURE WITH COMMON CENTS.** It's critical to maintain consistent spacing between drawer fronts, so rather than use a shim, the author used a pair of pennies between the faces to set the gap.

avoid taking up space that could otherwise be used for storage inside the drawer. I marked and drilled the positions of the holes, then installed the brackets and checked across all four to confirm that they were level.

I set the outer cabinets on the brackets and transferred the measurements for the plumbing onto the back of the center cabinet. After cutting the holes and checking the fit, I installed the center cabinet by carefully lowering it into place onto temporary supports. I then attached all three cases together by inserting bolts into the T-nuts. I screwed the outer cases onto the brackets and locked them into place. To draw the face frames tight, I also ran bolts through the face-frame edges.

I scribed the end panels to the wall and attached them with wood glue and brads. (The interior finished panels next to the center cabinet were cut and installed in the shop.) Now I was ready to finish the puzzle. I hung the doors, then attached each drawer face to its box with 1-in. #6 pan-head screws fitted through ¾-in. by ⅛-in. fender washers. I carefully adjusted the faces until they were even across the entire assembly. (Placing coins between the faces is a great way to maintain even margins between the elements.) Finally, I fit the central dummy panel that will conceal the sink and attached it to the outside cases by screwing it to the blocks above the center cabinet.

## IN A PERFECT WORLD, SCREWS WOULD BE ENOUGH

**I CALCULATED THAT THE CABINET** would weigh 207 lb. Add to this the concrete counter (which will sometimes be holding a full sink of water), the cabinet's contents, and the likelihood that someone, someday, will think that it makes sense to stand on the cabinet while changing a light bulb, and the total load could exceed 350 lb. For this job, I decided to use brackets rated for 330 lb. per pair, which I found at Häfele, the cabinet-hardware supply company. To counteract the shear, I bought 1-in. by 1-in. steel angle iron from my local welding shop. After cutting it to the width of each side cabinet, I drilled holes into one side and screwed the pieces to the wall against the underside of the cabinet.

# Yard-Sale Bureau Becomes a Bathroom Vanity

BY MIKE GUERTIN

One-of-a-kind bureaus are easy to find at yard sales, secondhand shops, and antique stores. They make unique bathroom or powder-room vanities and can cost hundreds of dollars less than commercially available cabinetry built to look like furniture. I've turned many bureaus into vanities, including two in my own house, with just simple modifications to the tops, backing panels, and drawers. Here are some tips for a successful conversion.

Ideally, you should select a bureau before installing the rough plumbing. This way, the drain and supply connections can be positioned to fit the bureau rather than requiring modifications later.

Choose a sink to suit both the size and the shape of the bureau top. Drop-in, undermount, and top-mount sinks are all suitable for bureau conversions.

Because of the space needed for the underside of the sink bowl and the plumbing, many faux-antique, store-bought vanities have fake drawer fronts that obviously aren't useful. You don't necessarily need to sacrifice the drawers on an antique bureau to the sink and plumbing; they can be modified to fit.

I make cardboard templates of the existing drawers and use a trial-and-error process to scribe the sides and the bottom panel precisely around the obstructions. Once the cardboard template fits, I cut

# SIMPLE MODIFICATIONS CREATE A SEAMLESS TRANSFORMATION

**ANY SINK WILL WORK,** but a drop-in style, as shown below, hides any imperfections in the cutout. I mark the opening on the bureau top, drill a starting hole in the waste area, and use a jigsaw to make the cutout. A reverse-toothed blade (teeth pointing down) helps to reduce tearout in the top surface.

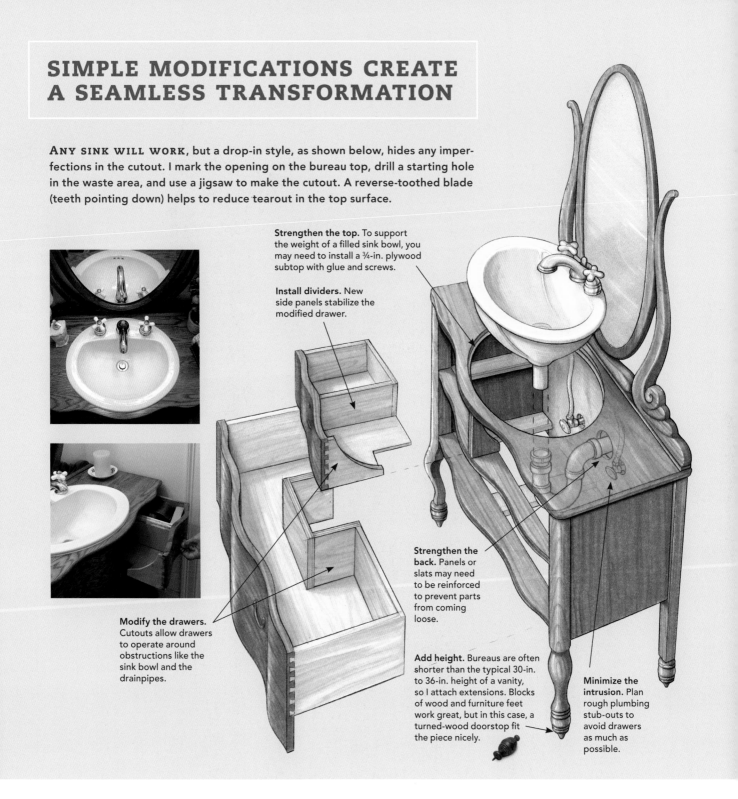

**Strengthen the top.** To support the weight of a filled sink bowl, you may need to install a ¾-in. plywood subtop with glue and screws.

**Install dividers.** New side panels stabilize the modified drawer.

**Strengthen the back.** Panels or slats may need to be reinforced to prevent parts from coming loose.

**Modify the drawers.** Cutouts allow drawers to operate around obstructions like the sink bowl and the drainpipes.

**Add height.** Bureaus are often shorter than the typical 30-in. to 36-in. height of a vanity, so I attach extensions. Blocks of wood and furniture feet work great, but in this case, a turned-wood doorstop fit the piece nicely.

**Minimize the intrusion.** Plan rough plumbing stub-outs to avoid drawers as much as possible.

---

the drawers to match and reinforce them with intermediate partitions. This way, I can retain 50 percent to 90 percent use of the drawers.

The veneers and glues used to make many old bureaus aren't intended for wet locations. To prevent

the risk of delamination, I strip off old finishes and coat the top with exterior-grade marine urethane or two-part acrylic urethane. The vertical surfaces can be finished with regular urethane or varnish.

# Break Out of the Bathroom Vanity Box

BY IAN INGERSOLL

Lately I've grown tired of vanity cabinets. Apparently I'm not alone, because in catalogs and showrooms I see more and more bathroom furniture: table-like vanities, stand-alone cabinets, little stands for serving up towels. But I didn't arrive at my design from the ranks of the avant-garde; rather, this vanity, with its gently tapered and splayed legs, is an outgrowth of years of working in the Shaker tradition.

I see it as a forward-looking nod to the Shaker washstand. I've also grown tired of cherry, a wood I feel furniture makers have worked to death. I made this vanity out of walnut, and a cheap grade at that, oxidized a deep, mocha brown with potassium permanganate (see the sidebar on p. 133). The vanity base fits comfortably under a solid-surface top and relies on a few simple design moves and the striking ebony-like finish. With this design, you won't need a fat wallet to make your bathroom look like a million bucks.

In designing the vanity, I had to consider a few issues particular to the genre. For height, I went with a fairly standard 33 in. For width, a 34-in. top felt right, and it allowed for two narrow drawers, one to either side of the bowl. The one caveat is that 34 in. is not a standard top size. You could adapt my design for either a 31-in. top or a 37-in. top, the two standard sizes closest to 34 in. Or you could have the top custom fabricated (see the sidebar on p. 129), as I did. Regardless of the width you choose, you may need a custom top to get one without the standard-issue integral backsplash.

Vanity tops are 22 in. deep, so to determine the overhang and the ultimate width of the table, I had to work back from 22 in. The key is to allow enough overhang in the rear so that the backsplash will sit flush against the wall and the legs will leave room for baseboard molding (see the bottom drawing on p. 130).

Even a vanity-as-table benefits from storage space. So I insisted on the two drawers, and I included a grate for a shelf. I'd used a similar floating grate on a kitchen island, and it seemed just right for this vanity.

To accommodate plumbing, I made the aprons deep enough to hide the sink bowl and most of the trap; a little chrome plumbing showing underneath keeps the vanity honest. You or your plumber can relocate the supply lines to run through or just below the rear apron. Either way, you won't see them from the front. As for moisture, a few coats of polyurethane over the permanganate finish should protect the wood surfaces for years. And compared with a closed-in cabinet, the open design of the legs and grate allow plenty of air circulation.

Constructing the vanity requires a trick or two, but it isn't difficult or especially time-consuming if

**THE FRONT APRON.** Rip and reglue to craft a front apron with flush drawers. Rip the apron at the top and bottom of the drawers (above). After jointing the ripped edges, cut the middle piece to make two drawer fronts; then glue and clamp the apron pieces together again (right). Cut the apron to length after glue-up. With a saw set to cut at 2 degrees, mark the length at the top of the apron (below). After the apron is glued in place, mark the upper outside corner of the drawer fronts and cut them to length with the saw set at 2 degrees (bottom right).

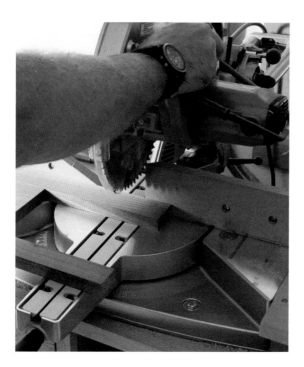

you take it in stages. Easy for me to say, since Pieter Mulder, one of the craftsmen I employ, built the prototype for me. But I think Pieter would agree.

## Vanity Is a Table

Not counting the floating grate or the backsplash, the essence of the vanity is four legs and four aprons, plus the two drawers. Make them in that order.

I needed to leave a full 16 in. for the sink bowl, which necessitated pushing the drawers against the tapered legs. An angled drawer front is scarcely harder to make than a straight-sided drawer front, and the slim line between the drawer front and the leg helps you read the legs as splayed, even though the angle is a mere 2 degrees. I had a guy working for me a while back, and his first run of supposedly vertical tables turned out splayed: He called it his fat-boy line of furniture, because it looked like someone heavy had sat on the tables. With the vanity, I intended the splay.

Mill the legs square and then cut the tapers. The taper on both the inside faces of the legs runs straight from the bottom of the apron to the foot of the leg

(see the drawing on p. 130). Save the scraps from your ripcuts and use them later as clamping pads when gluing the aprons to the legs. Cut the mortises perpendicular to the inside faces of the legs.

Mill the aprons long, and cut them to length with a chop saw set at 2 degrees off vertical. To figure the finished length of each apron, determine the distance between the legs at the top and add $1\frac{3}{8}$ in. on each side for tenons; for instance, Pieter cut the side aprons $17\frac{3}{4}$ in. long.

Before cutting the tenons, you need to rip and reglue the front apron for the two flush drawers. The front apron needs to begin a bit wider and longer than the other aprons because you'll lose two sawkerfs when you cut out the drawer fronts. Rip the apron proud of your lines, so you can joint the fresh edges before glue-up. The reglued apron will have a very close grain match despite the missing kerfs. Once the front apron has been glued together again, you can joint all four aprons at the same time.

Now you can cut all the tenons. Use a tablesaw with a dado set, cutting the shoulders first with the board flat over the dado set. Then cut the cheeks us-

## CHOOSING A SOLID-SURFACE VANITY TOP

**SOLID-SURFACE TOPS**, such as Corian®, are seamless, nonporous, and highly stain-resistant, but the reason I like them is that they look and feel good. You can order solid-surface tops from local hardware stores, building supply centers, or kitchen and bath shops. Corian is probably the best-known solid-surface top; others, all roughly the same, include Swanstone®, Avonite®, and Wilsonart®.

For the vanity, I chose a solid-surface top in ice white, with an integral 16-in. oval bowl. The solid-surface sheets I used were nominally ½ in. thick; I specified double-thick edges. Most fabricators will drill holes for the faucet and handles free of charge. I selected a polished chrome faucet and polished chrome lever handles with white porcelain inserts.

Regardless of the top you choose, be sure to have it on hand or know its dimensions with absolute certainty before you determine the exact dimensions of your base.

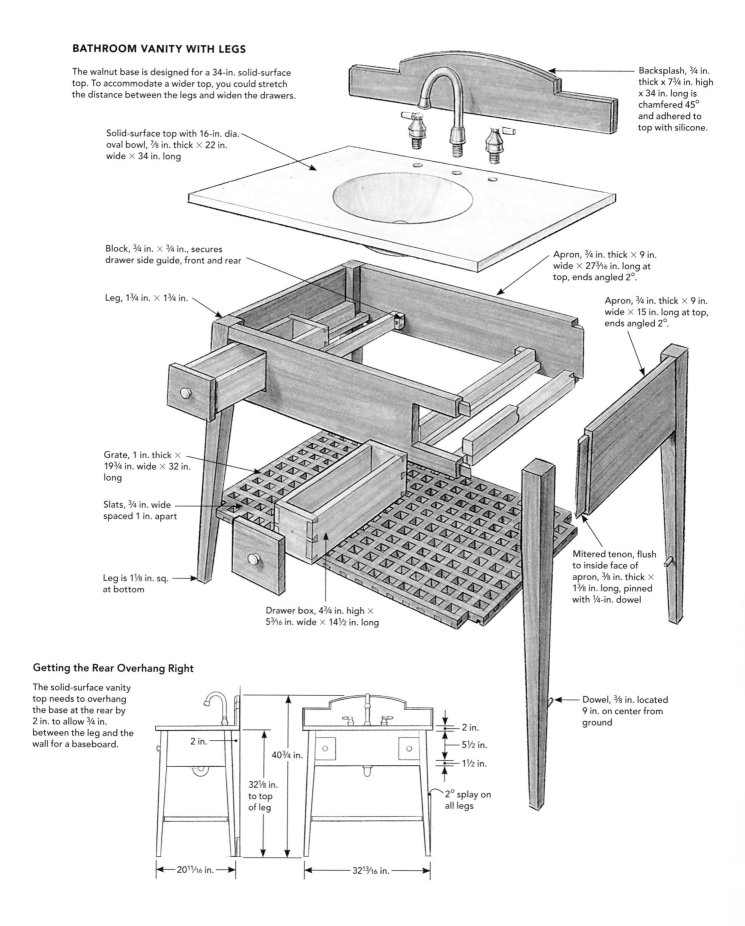

## BATHROOM VANITY WITH LEGS

The walnut base is designed for a 34-in. solid-surface top. To accommodate a wider top, you could stretch the distance between the legs and widen the drawers.

Backsplash, ¾ in. thick x 7¾ in. high x 34 in. long is chamfered 45° and adhered to top with silicone.

Solid-surface top with 16-in. dia. oval bowl, ⅞ in. thick × 22 in. wide × 34 in. long

Block, ¾ in. × ¾ in., secures drawer side guide, front and rear

Leg, 1¾ in. × 1¾ in.

Apron, ¾ in. thick × 9 in. wide × 27³⁄₁₆ in. long at top, ends angled 2°.

Apron, ¾ in. thick × 9 in. wide × 15 in. long at top, ends angled 2°.

Grate, 1 in. thick × 19¾ in. wide × 32 in. long

Slats, ¾ in. wide spaced 1 in. apart

Mitered tenon, flush to inside face of apron, ⅜ in. thick × 1⅜ in. long, pinned with ¼-in. dowel

Leg is 1⅛ in. sq. at bottom

Drawer box, 4¾ in. high × 5³⁄₁₆ in. wide × 14½ in. long

Dowel, ⅜ in. located 9 in. on center from ground

### Getting the Rear Overhang Right

The solid-surface vanity top needs to overhang the base at the rear by 2 in. to allow ¾ in. between the leg and the wall for a baseboard.

2 in.

40¾ in.

32⅛ in. to top of leg

2 in.

5½ in.

1½ in.

2° splay on all legs

20¹¹⁄₁₆ in.

32¹³⁄₁₆ in.

**FIRST CROSS-DADO A LONG BLANK USING A SIMPLE JIG.** With this jig you'll be able to index a series of consistent dadoes across a 1-in.-thick by 3-in.- or 4-in.- wide board.

## MAKING THE GRATE

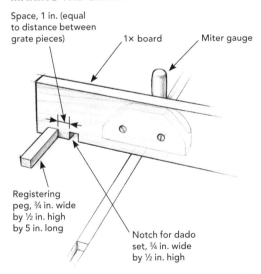

Space, 1 in. (equal to distance between grate pieces)

1× board

Miter gauge

Registering peg, ¾ in. wide by ½ in. high by 5 in. long

Notch for dado set, ¾ in. wide by ½ in. high

ing a miter gauge, with the boards standing on edge. Because the shoulders are cut 2 degrees off vertical, cutting the cheeks on edge will leave a triangle that must be pared out by hand.

Once you've cut the legs and aprons, you're ready to glue up the table. Leave the aprons a touch proud of the legs, and scrape and sand them flush. If, instead, the leg is proud of the apron, you'll run into trouble because you'll lose the crisp line of the leg as you sand it down. The 2-degree taper on the aprons will transfer to the legs, so you may want to beltsand or plane the tops of the legs flush with the top edges of the aprons. Sanding the legs flush with the apron will help the vanity top to sit flat. One nice thing

# A CLEVER WAY TO FLOAT A WOOD GRATE

I CONSIDERED SEVERAL WAYS OF ATTACHING THE GRATE to the legs, but settled on resting the grate on four dowels, one protruding from each leg (see the photo at right). With a ½-in. reveal between the grate and the legs and with the dowels half-hidden in notches in the underside of the grate, anyone walking up to the vanity will perceive the grate as floating. (Those who get down on their hands and knees and crawl around on your bathroom floor will have earned the right to know how the grate is attached.) Use ⅜-in. wood or metal dowels, set ⅝ in. into the leg and protruding 1 in. Be sure to drill the hole for the dowel parallel to the vanity top, not perpendicular to the splayed and tapered leg.

about the splayed legs and the floating grate is that you don't have to include the grate in the glue-up.

You can build the two drawer boxes any way you like; just be sure the inner sides avoid the sink bowl. Wait until the table is glued up to cut the drawer front to length. Mark the length of the top edge against the drawer opening, and use this mark to make a 2-degree cut.

Making the wood grate takes less time than you might think, as long as you don't attempt to cut and notch each piece individually. The trick is to cut a series of dadoes, half the thickness of the board, across a wide 1-in.-thick board. Then rip the board, which results in several identically notched strips indexed to fit together when arranged in a grid.

**RIP THE BLANK INTO NOTCHED STRIPS.** When you rip a really wide board into narrow strips, you have many chances to kick the board off square as you pass it through the saw, resulting in tapered strips that don't fit well together. You're better off ripping boards that are 3 in. or 4 in. wide.

For a grate that appears to float around the legs, first make a full rectangular grid and then cut away the corners with a jigsaw. Chisel the inside faces clean. The assembled grate can be sanded with a belt sander or sent through a thickness sander.

## Putting a Lid on It

Once you've assembled the legs and aprons, fitted the drawers, and built the grate, you're almost done. The next-to-last step is to install the solid-surface top onto the wood table. It's almost a non-event, a task best left undone until you're actually plumbing the vanity. A solid-surface top is quite heavy—it tends to stay where you put it—and the wood table needs to move under it, so the barest of connections is required. Simply run a bead of silicone along the top edge of the front apron, and lay the solid-surface top in place.

The backsplash is shaped from a 7¾-in.-wide piece of walnut. Cut it with a bandsaw, clean it up, and then use a chamfer bit on your router to bevel the edge.

The final step, I promise, is to attach the backsplash to the solid-surface top. With the vanity in place, affix the backsplash to the rear wall with silicone and run a bead of caulk between the backsplash and vanity top. Now you can admire your work, and then wash your hands.

## A RICH FINISH FOR POOR WOOD

THERE ARE ANY NUMBER OF DISASTER STORIES associated with the use of potassium permanganate as a finish, most having to do with turning something black that wasn't supposed to be.

A chemical that oxidizes wood to change its color, potassium permanganate is sold in water-soluble salt form. It is considered a toxin, though it is neither volatile, flammable, nor listed as a carcinogen. You should wear a respirator when mixing the salts and gloves when applying the finish. When purchasing potassium permanganate, ask for a Material Safety Data Sheet (MSDS) and expect to pay a hazardous-material shipping charge if you have it shipped to you.

Potassium permanganate reacts differently to different woods and at different dilutions, so always test it on some scrap. It dries in one to two hours, and it is very forgiving and uniform in darker shades, making it a good choice for inexpensive, poor quality woods, such as sappy walnut.

For the vanity, David Blakey, one of the finishers at my shop, applied three coats of potassium permanganate (1 tablespoon mixed with 1 quart of water) and then two coats of Minwax® Polyshade, a urethane with a tint to prevent UV damage to the oxidized finish.

# A Space-Saving Island with Drawers

BY JOSEPH B. LANZA

I recently renovated a carriage house that was to be used for entertaining or for extended stays from my clients' family. On the upper level, more than half of the 20-ft. by 24-ft. space was taken up by the kitchen. To make the kitchen efficient, the clients and I wanted the island to be a space for working as well as for gathering and eating.

A few issues came up as I designed the rest of the kitchen. For example, positioning the sink and the major appliances along the outside wall wouldn't leave much space for storage. To have room for seating, the island needed an overhanging counter on three sides, which left room for only two base cabinets. I knew that the big overhang would create space for drawers below the top, a detail seen on many tables. Tablestyle legs on an island of this size, though, would look bulky and would interfere with seating. My challenge became how to support drawers without legs. Here was my solution: Two plywood base cabinets with solid, substantial tops and backs support a frame of 5/4 poplar glued and screwed together and skinned with a piece of ½-in. birch plywood. This frame supports a countertop of solid 6/4 maple, which, in turn, stiffens and supports the frame. The frame carries the drawers on side-mount slides to save space. The base is covered with 4/4 walnut random-width beadboard, drawers, and door fronts.

**TOP DOES DOUBLE DUTY.** To get both seating and storage in this island, the top had to multitask. The key to its success is an open frame made of 5/4 poplar strong enough to support a cantilevered maple countertop, yet with space for six drawers. The addition of a layer of ½-in. plywood creates a structure stronger than the frame alone.

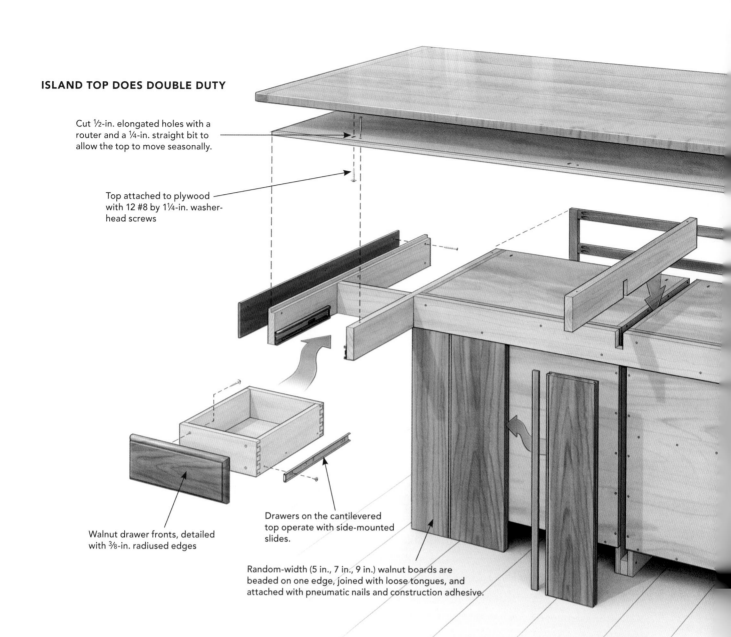

## ISLAND TOP DOES DOUBLE DUTY

Cut ½-in. elongated holes with a router and a ¼-in. straight bit to allow the top to move seasonally.

Top attached to plywood with 12 #8 by 1¼-in. washer-head screws

Walnut drawer fronts, detailed with ⅜-in. radiused edges

Drawers on the cantilevered top operate with side-mounted slides.

Random-width (5 in., 7 in., 9 in.) walnut boards are beaded on one edge, joined with loose tongues, and attached with pneumatic nails and construction adhesive.

**CHECK THE FIT.** Because the frame's strength depends on the locations and the tightness of the bridle joints, dry-fit the entire frame around the cabinets before applying glue.

**ADD THE TOP.** Once the frame is assembled, measure and cut a piece of ½-in. plywood that will strengthen the base for the solid maple countertop.

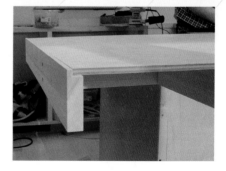

**EDGES CONCEALED.** Although the plywood is hidden by the drawers and trim, the author recessed the plywood into the frame and covered the sides with a band of poplar.

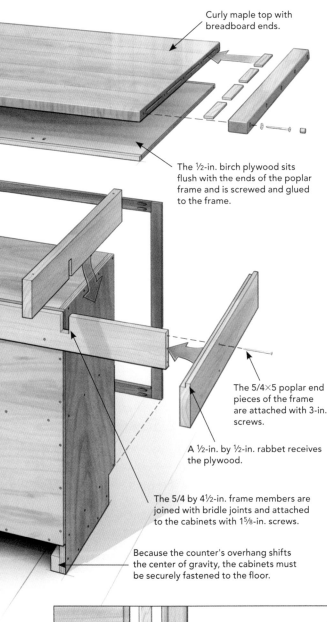

Curly maple top with breadboard ends.

The ½-in. birch plywood sits flush with the ends of the poplar frame and is screwed and glued to the frame.

The 5/4×5 poplar end pieces of the frame are attached with 3-in. screws.

A ½-in. by ½-in. rabbet receives the plywood.

The 5/4 by 4½-in. frame members are joined with bridle joints and attached to the cabinets with 1⅝-in. screws.

Because the counter's overhang shifts the center of gravity, the cabinets must be securely fastened to the floor.

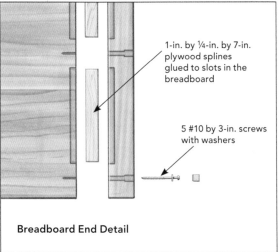

1-in. by ¼-in. by 7-in. plywood splines glued to slots in the breadboard

5 #10 by 3-in. screws with washers

**Breadboard End Detail**

## Start with the Boxes

I'm a big fan of simple cabinet boxes, and these boxes fit that category perfectly. I often use ¾-in. birch plywood, and I glue, nail, and screw the butt joints together. I wanted these two cabinets to be able to support the big maple top, so I stiffened them with ¾-in. backs and full (rather than strip) tops. One cabinet holds the microwave, and the other features a drawer above a pair of doors.

At the site, I marked the locations for the boxes and screwed 2× cleats to the floor just inside their footprints at each end. Between where the two cabinets would rest I anchored another cleat the same thickness as the frame and screwed the cabinets to the cleats.

## Integrate the Frame with the Boxes

To support the top and to house the drawers, I made a frame of 5/4×5 poplar that would extend beyond the cabinets approximately 14 in. To make a more positive connection with the plywood subtop, I cut a ½-in.-deep rabbet along the edges of both end pieces and ripped the remaining pieces down to 4½ in. I cut bridle joints at the appropriate points and attached the frame with glue and screws. I cut the plywood to size and screwed and glued it to the top of the frame.

## Final Assembly

Back at the site, I installed the face frames and attached the beadboard. After installing the drawers and their Blum undermount slides on the work side, I hung the doors and the drawer fronts. On the seating side of the island I installed the drawers with Accuride®-style side-mount slides. I completed the job by finishing both the walnut base and the maple top with three coats of Ceramithane®, a waterborne urethane.

# Build a Kitchen Island

BY RICK GEDNEY

The function of a modern kitchen island can be traced to the familiar kitchen worktable that's been helping families run the household and prepare meals for generations. An island's job is even tougher, though: A table from the eighteenth or nineteenth century didn't need to be a space for making pizza, checking email, or stir-frying. It also didn't have to integrate pipes, ducts, and wires.

I was recently called to a client's house for a full kitchen remodel. The young family wanted to renovate their existing, space-challenged galley kitchen, turning it into a wide-open room with an eat-at island. We looked at the available space and decided a single-level island with a farm sink made the most sense.

One often-overlooked item with island installations is how different floor coverings transition

**WORK FROM THE END.** With the position of the sink's overhead light as a starting point, use the kitchen designer's measured drawings to determine the end of the island. Measure from the wall cabinets to create a parallel line that the island will follow.

**FIND MIDDLE GROUND.** Many installers find the highest point of the floor to reference cabinet height, and then shim up the cabinets that sit on low spots. A better option is to find a cabinet at average height and then shim the low cabinets up and plane the high cabinets down. Shimming and planing should be minimal.

**CENTER THE SINK.** Using a pair of levels, transfer to the floor the location of the light fixture centered over the sink. This becomes the starting point for the layout.

around the cabinets. On this project, we had to make an attractive transition between the wide pine floors in the adjacent living areas and the new kitchen's tile floor. We opted to make the transition at the end of the island and run the wide pine under the eating area. This seemed like the most logical spot to transition between the two types of flooring.

The installation of this island was pretty typical, although the open ceiling in the basement made running pipes and wires to the island a little easier. In this case, the plumber and electrician decided it would be best to do their rough-ins after the cabinets were installed, although such a process varies from one job to the next. When I'm designing a kitchen island, I always get the general contractor and the subcontractors involved as soon as we have preliminary drawings because plumbing, ventilation, and electrical requirements can make some designs unworkable with a typical budget.

**CHECK ACROSS THE GAP.** Where there's a gap in the island's cabinet run for a dishwasher or other appliance, use a long level to ensure that both cabinets are at the same height. Check front and back to confirm that the cabinet tops are in the same plane. Also make sure the cabinets are spread at the proper distance and their sides are parallel.

## Start with a Focal Point, Then Follow the Plans

Light fixtures are typically centered over sinks and appliances, so this is a logical starting point for establishing the cabinet layout. From there, move left and right according to the plans, accounting for discrepancies in floor height as you move (see the photos on p. 139). With the cabinets aligned, screwed together, and at a consistent height, they can be fastened to the floor.

**LOWER THE HIGH CABINETS.** Using a level that spans from a high cabinet to one already at the correct height, center the bubble, and adjust your compass scribes so that they reflect the height difference. Use the same tool to mark the base of the cabinet for planing.

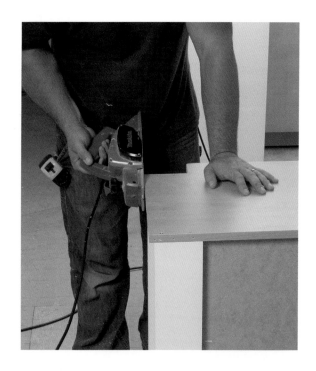

**ADJUST THE HEIGHT.** A few strokes with a power plane quickly remove enough stock to level the cabinet. This planer can remove about 1/32 in. with each pass while providing a smooth finish. Deeper passes leave a rough surface. Planing should be limited to a maximum of about 3/8 in.

**CHECK ONE MORE TIME FOR INCONSISTENT HEIGHT.** After the cabinet bottom is trimmed, put the cabinet in place, and check for level side to side and front to back. If necessary, make further adjustments with shims or planing until the cabinet is level in all directions.

**FASTEN TO THE FLOOR.** After two or three cabinets are screwed to each other, the cabinets are screwed to the floor. Drill pilot holes at an angle with a 7/32-in. twist bit, and then use 2½-in. square-drive screws to hold the cabinets to the floor.

## Create a Seating Area

Rather than having extradeep or extrawide boxes, semicustom cabinets often have extended side panels for scribing to walls or other cabinets. These panels often work in conjunction with factory-finished plywood and solid hardwood to cover cabinet backs and empty cavities. The built-in eating area on this island is defined with a plywood panel that matches the cabinets. These additional parts are cut to size before they're fit and fastened.

**TRIM FACTORY-FINISHED PANELS ON SITE.** Using a track-guided saw, cut a plywood panel to form one side of the island's eating area (left). Cut it with a 45-degree bevel to correspond to a bevel on the cabinet's side panel.

**GLUE MITERED JOINTS.** The end and back panels meet with a mitered joint. A thick bead of wood glue prevents the mitered joint from opening with changes in humidity (left). While the glue dries, the joint is held together with 2-in.-wide masking tape (above).

**BLOCKING REINFORCES THE PANEL.** Use scraps of hardwood or plywood blocking to reinforce the eating area's plywood panels. Pocket screws are a strong, efficient way to make these connections. Previously installed cabinets make a great workbench for drilling pocket holes.

**FASTEN THE BLOCKING.** Using 1¼-in. coarse-thread pocket-hole screws, fasten blocking between the top of the plywood and the adjacent cabinet backs. The blocking prevents the plywood panel from warping.

**LOCATE THE LEGS, AND CUT THEM TO LENGTH.** A pair of legs support the eating area's overhanging countertop. Use a pair of levels as straightedges to position the legs in plane with the cabinets.

**ATTACH THE LEGS TO THE FLOOR.** After drilling a hole in the center of the leg, fasten the leg to a 2½-in. drywall screw that's been cut off with lineman's pliers (left). This anchors the leg in place without visible fasteners (below).

**TURN EACH LEG UPSIDE DOWN** over where it will be installed so that it can be marked for trimming on a miter saw. Cut the long part of the leg to keep the top consistent.

**INSTALL AN APRON.** Secured with pocket screws, a 2-in.-wide apron under the overhanging countertop supports the legs and provides a finished look. A 6-in. apron on the back of the island holds a receptacle.

**ADD BRACING.** Two-in.-wide stretchers attach the apron to the back of the cabinets, while angle braces keep the corners square. Both types of bracing are held in place with 1¼-in. coarse-thread pocket screws.

## Finishing Touches

The finishing touches depend on the individual island, but most islands need drawer and cabinet pulls and some way to hide the obvious seams between cabinets. Appliances and fixtures may be installed now or after the top is in place, depending on the appliances. Once the cabinets are finished, it's time for the fabricator to measure for the countertop.

HIDE THE SEAMS AND SCREWS. The seam at the end of the island where the two cabinets meet is often hidden with a wine rack, bookshelves, or panels. This island has a pair of panels that mimic the cabinet doors (above). The seam between panels is offset from the cabinet seam, locking the cabinets together. Screws installed from the back side are hidden from view (left).

CUT THE FARM-SINK OPENING. Once the cleats that support the sink top are cut and secured to the sides of this cabinet, the installer cuts the blank panel at the front of the cabinet with a jigsaw (left) and cleans it up with a rasp (right). When finished, the sink will be flush with the cabinet.

# TIME FOR TEMPLATING

**WITH THE CABINETS IN PLACE,** the eating area finished, and the farm sink installed, it's time for the stone fabricator to create a template of the counter-top. Decisions about thickness, the way the top overhangs the cabinets, and edge treatments should all be decided by this point.

# A Clever Kitchen Built-In

BY NANCY R. HILLER

**M**odern kitchens are made for storage, but it never seems to be sufficient. Recently, my company built a cabinet to provide generous storage on a shallow section of wall in our clients' kitchen. It was space that normally would have gone to waste because it was too shallow for stock cabinets.

The inspiration for this custom-made cabinet came from a traditional piece of British furniture known as a Welsh dresser. In use since the seventeenth century, the dresser originally provided the main storage in a kitchen; built-in cabinets did not become the norm until the early twentieth century. More commonly known in the United States by the less-elegant term *hutch*, the dresser typically has a shallow, open upper section that sits on a partially enclosed base. The dresser described here also exemplifies the sort of planning, production, and installation essential for genuinely custom built-in cabinets.

## A Strategy for Storage That Doesn't Waste Space

The kitchen had a section of unused wall about 11 ft. long, which I thought could be used for storage and display space without impeding traffic flow. Although 1 ft. of depth is shallow for a base cabinet,

it is enough to hold a surprising variety of kitchen wares: cookbooks, decorative china, coffee mugs, small mixing bowls, jars of beans or pasta. Knowing that one of my clients had grown up in England and would be familiar with Welsh dressers, I suggested a similar cabinet with more-contemporary lines, customized for her family's budget and for the available space.

The upper sections would have open shelves, but the base cabinets would be enclosed with doors and drawers to keep their contents free of the dust and debris that collect at a kitchen's edges. Enclosing the lower sections also would give a nice visual weight to the wall without making it appear too heavy. The break between base and upper cabinets would be at 32 in., not the typical kitchen-counter height of 36 in., because I wanted this piece to look more like furniture than a regular kitchen cabinet.

## Building Smaller Components Makes the Project Easier

The six-piece unit is divided into three uppers and three bases for ease of production, delivery, and installation (see the drawing on the facing page). To make the six plywood cases and the solid-maple counter resemble a single piece of cabinetry, I used a complete maple face frame on the center section

**MORE PARTS MAKE CONSTRUCTION EFFICIENT.** This type of modular cabinet construction allows a majority of the assembly work to be done in the shop. Consequently, I get more control over the processes and their costs.

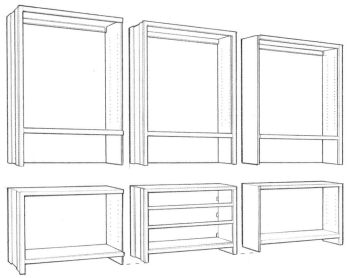

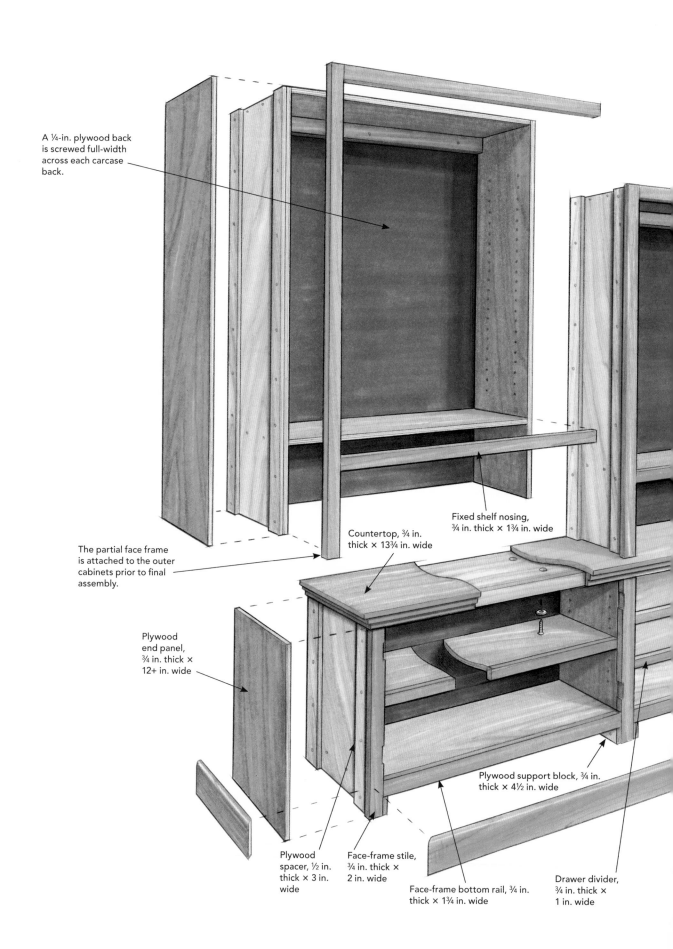

A ¼-in. plywood back is screwed full-width across each carcase back.

The partial face frame is attached to the outer cabinets prior to final assembly.

Fixed shelf nosing, ¾ in. thick × 1¾ in. wide

Countertop, ¾ in. thick × 13¾ in. wide

Plywood end panel, ¾ in. thick × 12+ in. wide

Plywood support block, ¾ in. thick × 4½ in. wide

Plywood spacer, ½ in. thick × 3 in. wide

Face-frame stile, ¾ in. thick × 2 in. wide

Face-frame bottom rail, ¾ in. thick × 1¾ in. wide

Drawer divider, ¾ in. thick × 1 in. wide

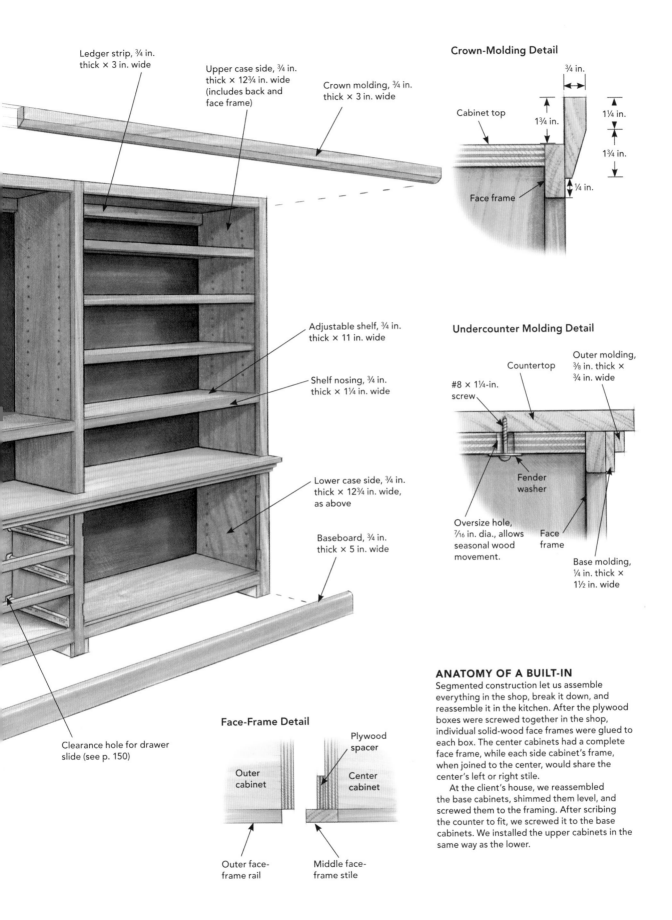

Ledger strip, ¾ in. thick × 3 in. wide

Upper case side, ¾ in. thick × 12¾ in. wide (includes back and face frame)

Crown molding, ¾ in. thick × 3 in. wide

Adjustable shelf, ¾ in. thick × 11 in. wide

Shelf nosing, ¾ in. thick × 1¼ in. wide

Lower case side, ¾ in. thick × 12¾ in. wide, as above

Baseboard, ¾ in. thick × 5 in. wide

Clearance hole for drawer slide (see p. 150)

## Crown-Molding Detail

¾ in.

Cabinet top

1¾ in.

1¼ in.

1¾ in.

¼ in.

Face frame

## Undercounter Molding Detail

Outer molding, ⅜ in. thick × ¾ in. wide

Countertop

#8 × 1¼-in. screw

Fender washer

Oversize hole, ⁷⁄₁₆ in. dia., allows seasonal wood movement.

Face frame

Base molding, ¼ in. thick × 1½ in. wide

## Face-Frame Detail

Plywood spacer

Outer cabinet

Center cabinet

Outer face-frame rail

Middle face-frame stile

## ANATOMY OF A BUILT-IN

Segmented construction let us assemble everything in the shop, break it down, and reassemble it in the kitchen. After the plywood boxes were screwed together in the shop, individual solid-wood face frames were glued to each box. The center cabinets had a complete face frame, while each side cabinet's frame, when joined to the center, would share the center's left or right stile.

At the client's house, we reassembled the base cabinets, shimmed them level, and screwed them to the framing. After scribing the counter to fit, we screwed it to the base cabinets. We installed the upper cabinets in the same way as the lower.

of the upper and lower casework and a partial face frame on each end. The end cases would butt tightly against the center unit and share its face-frame stiles to make the unit appear as one piece (see the drawing on pp. 148–149).

Although 10-in. slides are available for many purposes and would have been ideal for this job, they are rated for drawers only up to approximately 2 ft. wide. For smooth operation, I needed hardware designed for oversize openings. Given the location of the adjacent door casing, which limited the cabinet's depth to a maximum of 12¾ in., and a design that called for inset drawer faces, we needed to create ¼ in. of additional depth to accommodate the 12-in. slides by routing out the plywood cabinet back in those locations.

For ease of production, I typically use a full-width applied back on built-in cabinets rather than rabbeting the cabinet sides to accept the back. Scribed on site, a finished end covers the seam between the cabinet and the ¼-in. back. After cutting biscuit slots to join the case sides to the tops, I used cleats fastened with glue and brads or screws to support

the case bottoms. The biscuit- and cleat-supported butt joints were reinforced with 1½-in. screws once the casework was put together.

As we assembled the cases, I checked for square and twist. I also cleaned off squeezed-out glue before it dried.

## Solid-Wood Parts Need Special Consideration

Depending on the finish, I use either mortise-and-tenon joinery or pocket screws to assemble face frames before gluing them to carcases. Although pocket screws are quick and simple, I don't think the joint is as immobile as a glued mortise and tenon. Although a hairline gap isn't as noticeable in natural wood, I've learned the hard way not to use pocket screws for painted work that needs to look seamless. For this project, once the face frames were pocket-screwed, we glued and clamped them to the carcases.

The solid-maple counter was made by edge-joining two or three full-length boards. To increase the glue surface and to keep the boards even during clamping, I used biscuit joints about every 18 in. along the

# DRAWER SIZE AND WEIGHT DETERMINE DRAWER SLIDE HARDWARE

A DRAWER THAT'S 40 IN. WIDE REQUIRES SPECIAL SLIDES to withstand the stresses placed on it when it's fully extended. However, the full-extension, heavy-duty 12-in. drawer slides from Accuride (model 3640; www.accuride.com) that I chose turned out to be ¼ in. longer than the inside of the base cabinets. Fortunately, cutting a hole in the cabinet's back (see the photo at right) made just enough space.

To install the drawers, we hang the drawer box first and apply the face later (see the photo on p. 153). Typically, we hang the box with special low-profile screws that can be purchased with the drawer hardware. The box should be hung initially about ⅛ in. behind its final position. In this instance, we were working with ¾-in.-thick applied drawer faces, so the box was set back ⅞ in.

**FIRST ASSEMBLY IS DONE IN THE SHOP FOR A BETTER FINAL FIT.** After Jerry Nees glued the center face frame to the center cabinet, he clamped the base cabinets together in the shop. The left and right portions of the face frame then can be scribed to fit and glued to their respective cabinets. The process is repeated for the upper cabinets.

## SOLID DETAILS FOR LONG-LASTING DOORS

For most cabinet doors, I make stiles and rails from stock that's slightly thicker than ¾ in. I prefer to use mortise-and-tenon joinery (see the drawing at right), but cope-and-stick is also a viable option (see the drawing below). I cut the grooves and tenons on the tablesaw, using a dado blade and (for the tenons) a sliding miter gauge. I use a ⁵⁄₁₆-in.-wide mortise-and-tenon joint; I have found that my mortising machine's ⁵⁄₁₆-in.-dia. auger bit and hollow chisel are less likely to break from overheating than are ¼-in. tools. My door panels are typically solid wood. If the groove is ½ in. deep, I make the panel ⅛ in. less all around to allow for some expansion. In summer, when the relative humidity is high here in Indiana, I make the panels extend closer to ⁷⁄₁₆ in. into a ½-in.-deep groove.

### Cope-and-Stick Option

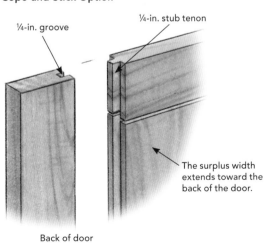

¼-in. groove

¼-in. stub tenon

The surplus width extends toward the back of the door.

Back of door

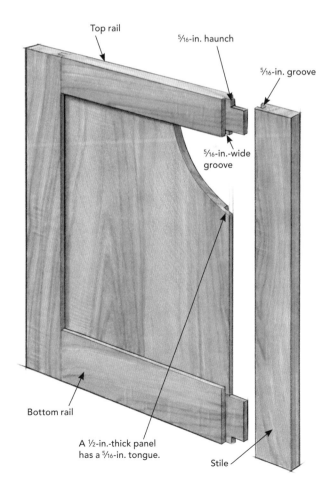

Top rail

⁵⁄₁₆-in. haunch

⁵⁄₁₆-in. groove

⁵⁄₁₆-in.-wide groove

Bottom rail

A ½-in.-thick panel has a ⁵⁄₁₆-in. tongue.

Stile

length. I determined the approximate location of the finished end so that I could avoid the nightmare of exposing a biscuit when I made the final cut. I sand and finish counters in the shop before I scribe and install them.

When I make cabinet doors, I keep the stock as thick as possible, at least ¾ in. and ideally ⅞ in. I flatten door stock on the jointer, then run it through the thickness planer to ensure that it is flat, square-edged, and uniform thickness. Using bar clamps rather than pipe clamps can help keep doors flat. I lay the door directly on the clamp-bar surface so I can detect any deflection and clamp the door to the bar using smaller clamps if necessary. I check for square by comparing diagonal measurements and hold a straightedge across the top and bottom of the frame to ensure that the rail and stile joints are glued up flat, not bowed. I also check for twist, either by sighting across the bare surface of the door or with the aid of winding sticks. Finally, I check the back of the door to make sure the panel is centered in the frame, and I adjust it if necessary by applying pressure with a wide chisel.

When the doors are dry, I rough-fit them to the cabinet openings using a handplane or a tablesaw. Then I rout and chisel mortises for the butt hinges on the cabinets' face frames; the mortises in the doors will come later.

Next, I install the case backs and the solid ledgers. These hanging strips are screwed not just through the ¼-in. plywood cabinet back, but directly through the top, the sides, or both. If the strips go only through the back and the back should somehow detach from the case, the entire assembly could fall forward, causing damage and possibly injury.

## Installation Starts at the Highest Point of the Floor

Because this design called for an applied base molding, I could shim the casework up to level and count on the baseboard to hide the shims. I began from the high point on the floor and shimmed the cases up

to level as necessary. The sections also were clamped together, so I could treat the three cabinets as a single unit if the wall behind them wasn't flat.

I use solid wood for counters because it generally holds up better than plywood and looks better with wear. When a solid counter is attached to a plywood case, the wood has to be able to move with changes in relative humidity. I set the counter in place and scribe as necessary, then attach it with screws in oversize holes that allow for wood movement.

As with the bases, I scribe the right face-frame stile to conform to irregularities in the wall, then screw together the upper units to form a single assembly before attaching it to the rear wall. No shimming is necessary because these upper cases are placed on a surface that should be level. I scribe the finished ends as needed and glue them in place. I also sand the face-frame edges flush if necessary.

## Hang the Doors and Drawers after the Casework Is Locked In

After applying the baseboard and crown molding, we work on the doors. For inset applications, I like to plane doors and drawer faces to size after installing the casework. Although this technique is unconventional, I find it more efficient. Once in their final position, cabinets don't always sit quite the way they did in the ideal conditions of the shop, so postponing this final fitting until the installation is complete means the work is done only once.

After shimming the doors in place with the proper margins (about 3/32 in. for stain grade, more for painted work), I mark the positions of the hinge mortises on the door stiles. Once marked, the door is clamped in a vise or on sawhorses, where I rout the mortises and mount the hinges. Once the door is rehung, I do a final fitting with a handplane.

Setting the drawers is the final stage. After finalizing the fit, I use a pair of screws and fender washers to hold the drawer face in position. Once I'm satisfied with the fit, I drive in four additional screws to lock the face to the drawer box.

## DRAWER CONSTRUCTION AND INSTALLATION: HANG THE BOX, THEN ATTACH THE FACE

I usually make drawers from ½-in. solid stock and dovetail the corners; it's a joinery option that my customers expect. (For less-expensive projects, I use biscuits or a rabbeted joint, as shown in the detail drawings below.) I groove the inside faces of the front and sides to accept the drawer bottom (I use ⅜-in.- or ½-in.-thick plywood for the bottoms of extra-wide drawers to prevent them from sagging). I also rip the back even with the top face of the drawer bottom so that I can slide in the bottom once the drawer sides are glued. Securing the bottom with small screws (but no glue) provides the option of a removable drawer bottom.

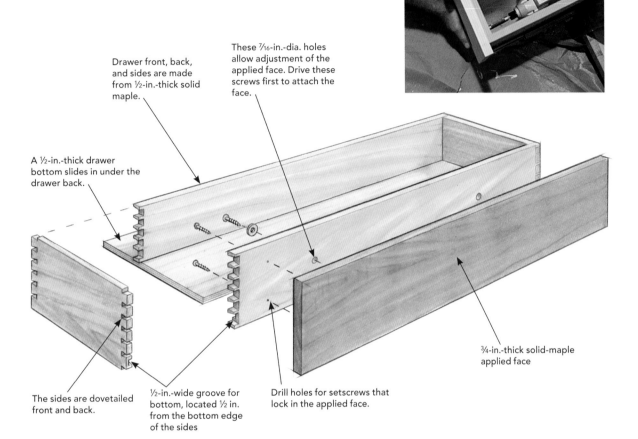

Drawer front, back, and sides are made from ½-in.-thick solid maple.

These ⁷⁄₁₆-in.-dia. holes allow adjustment of the applied face. Drive these screws first to attach the face.

A ½-in.-thick drawer bottom slides in under the drawer back.

The sides are dovetailed front and back.

½-in.-wide groove for bottom, located ½ in. from the bottom edge of the sides

Drill holes for setscrews that lock in the applied face.

¾-in.-thick solid-maple applied face

**Rabbet-Joint Option**

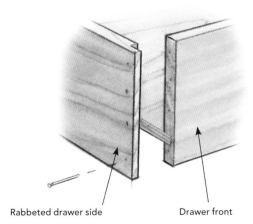

Rabbeted drawer side

Drawer front

**Biscuit-Joint Option**

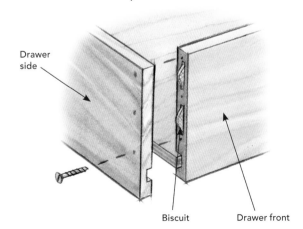

Drawer side

Biscuit

Drawer front

# Countertops

# A Designer's Guide to Countertops

BY JAMIE GOLD

There is no one-size-fits-all countertop for every kitchen, just as there is no one-size-fits-all kitchen for every home. When I began working as a designer close to a decade ago, most clients came to me wanting granite countertops. They ogled the large island covered in granite that we had on display—where no one ever cooked, chopped vegetables, mixed drinks, did homework, worked on art projects, or cleaned up after dinner.

Looking rich and beautiful is easy if you never do a day's work. It's harder for countertops subjected to the rigors of a family's daily living, especially spills, splatters, and flying projectiles. I design kitchens with an approach I call "sensible style." Its first principle is that your kitchen needs to fit how you really live.

The second sensible-style principle is that your new kitchen should honor the home it's being installed in; this means that your new countertops should complement the overall style and materials of the areas that surround the kitchen, as well as those in the kitchen itself. I've seen too many homeowners—and even some industry pros—choose a countertop without considering its maintenance requirements, durability, material properties such as softness or porosity, warranty, or even the way a pattern might play against neighboring surfaces such as kitchen cabinetry and flooring. My goal here is to help you avoid making such design mistakes.

## Establish a Design Process

Kitchen countertops should never be chosen on the basis of looks alone. First, consider the needs and the lifestyle of your family. Take into account habits and any physical limitations. Once you've done that, then you'll be ready to choose the type of material that will top your cabinets for the next 10 or 20 years.

The first elements to consider when choosing the look you want for your tops are the other major surfaces in the kitchen. I often start with the floor, which may extend beyond the kitchen and, in a remodel, may already be in place. Cabinets and appliances are also major aesthetic considerations. What is their color, style, and pattern? Is there just one cabinet finish to coordinate with, or several? (I keep a consistent top if the cabinet finishes vary.) How will the appliances look next to the tops? Is there too much contrast, or not enough?

Regardless of whether you pick color A or pattern B, you need to choose the type of material before the cabinetry design is completed. Your countertops may require special sink accommodations, or supports may need to be factored into the cabinet design and construction.

**STYLE AND USE ARE KEY.** In this midcentury San Diego kitchen designed by the author, the architect-homeowner, and a colleague, family-friendly engineered stone was used—also known as quartz—for the countertops. Its soft color and pebbly pattern coordinate handsomely with the floors' driftwood-gray finish, the glossy-white cabinets, and the oceanic touches throughout the surrounding spaces. The material evokes the nearby tide pools, where the family enjoys walking and which are visible from the adjacent living room.

In many of the spaces I design from scratch, cabinets are chosen first, then countertops and appliances, then flooring, then wall coverings. Other designers start with flooring and work their way up to the counters. The order is less important than taking a holistic approach.

## Matching the Top to the Use

Not all kitchens are used the same way. Some functionality issues I ask clients about include the

reduced vision, a balance impairment, or a memory limitation?

Homes with seniors can benefit from an acrylic or acrylic-blend countertop such as Corian or Avonite. These surfaces feel softer when struck by someone with depth-perception or balance problems, and they are reparable if a shaking hand with a knife misses the cutting board or a memory-challenged user sets a hot pot down on the bare surface. These materials are also nonporous, which reduces the risk of food contamination, and they are maintenance-free.

Because of its durability, low maintenance, and stain resistance, I often specify engineered stone for families with active children. An acrylic material can fit the bill, too, given its reparability. Porcelain- and ceramic-slab tops are also good family-friendly alternatives for their durability and minimal maintenance demands.

## Create a Cohesive Style

Kitchens tend to fall into one of four primary styles: traditional, contemporary or modern, transitional, and eclectic. Transitional kitchens are my favorite, as they blend many of the classic elements of traditional kitchens, such as crown molding and decorative hardware, with the simpler aesthetic of modern kitchens, such as simple hardware and streamlined, nonfussy door styles.

The countertop you choose should fit the overall style of the space. For example, wood can be butcher block for a casual transitional kitchen's food-prep area, or it can be elegant planks for a more formal buffet. Glass can be a slab for a contemporary cooking zone, or it can be a recycled blend for an eclectic focal-point bar. Metal options include zinc or copper for a traditional space, or stainless steel for a contemporary kitchen with next to no upkeep. Stone, such as marble, soapstone, or granite, is common for a traditional home whose owners don't mind the extra care. Quartz can be a good choice for the working surfaces of just about any style of kitchen, given the wide range of solids and patterns available.

type of food preparation and cooking they do on a regular basis. I ask how often they entertain, and if they do so formally or casually. I ask where in the kitchen they like to chop vegetables, trim meat, or mix drinks. I also want to know if they help children with homework in the kitchen, or bathe pets or babies, or fold laundry.

It's also important to ask user-oriented questions. For instance, does anyone who uses the kitchen have

# EIGHT GREAT COUNTERTOPS

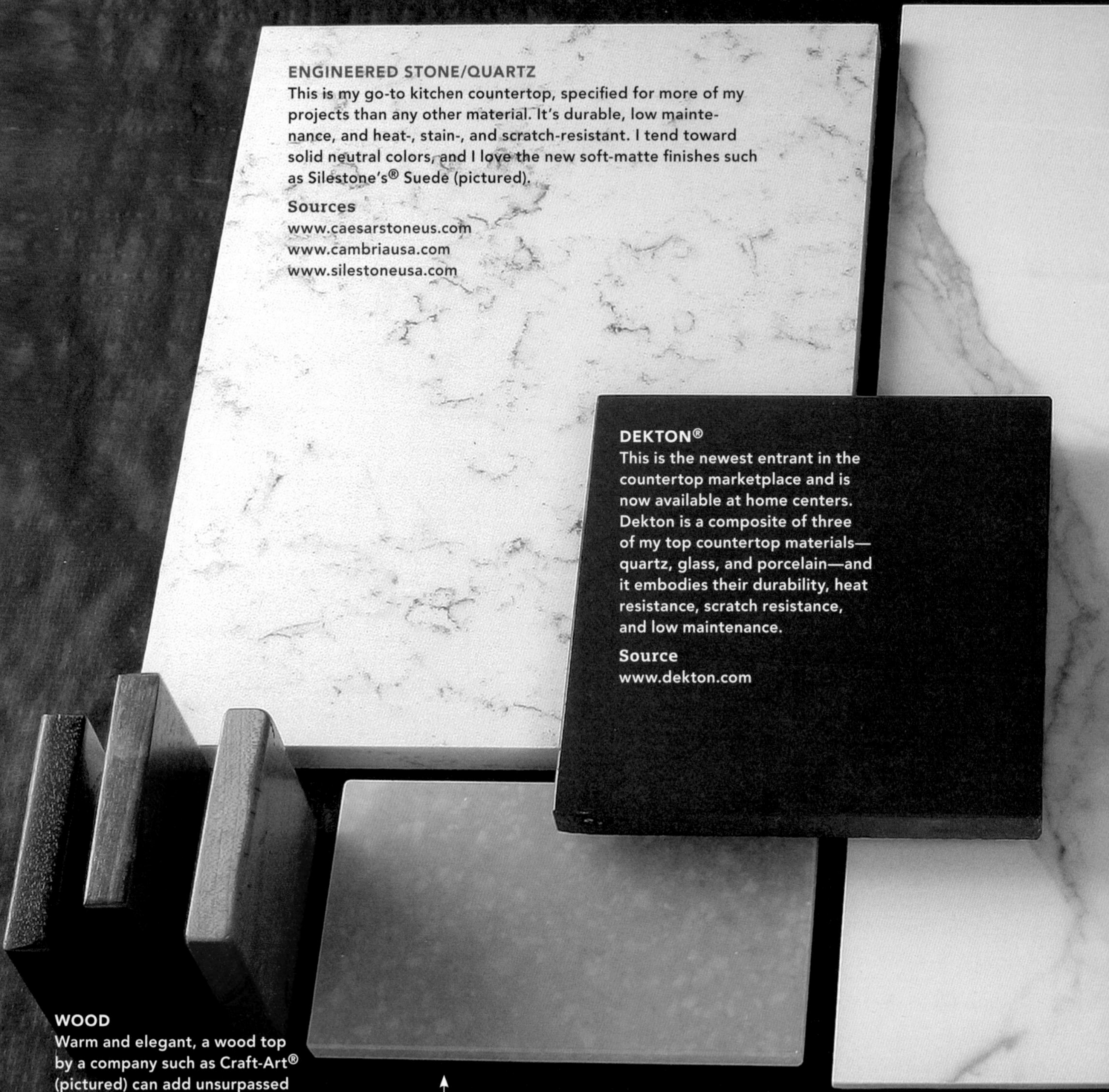

### ENGINEERED STONE/QUARTZ

This is my go-to kitchen countertop, specified for more of my projects than any other material. It's durable, low maintenance, and heat-, stain-, and scratch-resistant. I tend toward solid neutral colors, and I love the new soft-matte finishes such as Silestone's® Suede (pictured).

**Sources**
www.caesarstoneus.com
www.cambriausa.com
www.silestoneusa.com

### DEKTON®

This is the newest entrant in the countertop marketplace and is now available at home centers. Dekton is a composite of three of my top countertop materials—quartz, glass, and porcelain—and it embodies their durability, heat resistance, scratch resistance, and low maintenance.

**Source**
www.dekton.com

### WOOD

Warm and elegant, a wood top by a company such as Craft-Art® (pictured) can add unsurpassed beauty to a kitchen. I adore the look of wood countertops—particularly walnut on painted cabinets in a traditional kitchen. I'm less enamored with wood in food-prep or cooking zones.

**Sources**
www.craft-art.com
www.glumber.com (Grothouse)
www.jaaronwoodcountertops.com

### SOLID-SURFACE ACRYLIC AND ACRYLIC BLENDS

Tops such as Avonite (pictured) have a soft, low-glare, easy-care surface ideal for aging-in-place kitchens. I also like the material's seamless appearance. This material does have a few downsides: It can be scratched or scorched easily, and it rarely succeeds at looking as good as natural materials. Also, its cost is comparable to that of granite or quartz.

**Sources**
www.avonitesurfaces.com (Avonite)
www.corian.com
www.staron.com

## SLAB GLASS
Glass is extremely durable; it's heat- and damage-resistant with normal use. It's also a surface that can add exceptional drama to a kitchen, especially when it's underlit. Its major downside is cost, which puts it out of reach for projects that would use it for anything other than a small accent.

**Source**
www.thinkglass.com

## CONCRETE
Concrete is versatile and comes in virtually any color combination and pattern. Slab concrete, made by manufacturers such as the Concrete Collaborative (pictured), is nearly flawless in appearance. I like its industrial look for contemporary kitchens, but not its need for regular sealing.

**Sources**
www.concrete-collaborative.com
www.polycor.com (KarmaStone)

## PORCELAIN AND CERAMIC SLABS
Recently, I came across an Italian line, Iris (pictured), that looks like marble, but without its softness or porosity. There is also a new Iron Series from Spain's TheSize. Like any porcelain or ceramic surface, these countertops are durable and low maintenance. You now also can have an integral sink in the same pattern if you'd like, but the only edge profile offered is a bevel.

**Sources**
www.thesize.es
www.tpbarcelona.com
www.transceramica.com (Iris)

## RECYCLED GLASS
Recycled-glass countertops by companies such as Vetrazzo® (pictured) are made from bottles, windows, and other castoffs blended with cement to create smooth slabs with fun backstories. Because most of it needs to be sealed, I like this dramatic material as a focal-point countertop away from food-prep or cooking zones.

**Sources**
www.eos-surfaces.com (GEOS)
www.icestoneusa.com
www.vetrazzo.com

159

Finally, there's concrete, which can be poured or installed as a slab.

You also need to choose the right color, finish, and pattern to work with your kitchen's overall style and adjacent materials. I like to pull a dominant color from the floor for the countertop or go with a pattern or solid that will complement it. If everything's a focal point, nothing's a focal point.

Kitchens with high-gloss, solid-colored cabinets—white is popular—pair well with either low-sheen or textured tops. If the floor is glossy concrete or terrazzo, I opt for a top with some texture, such as a linen-look porcelain slab, to make the space feel less slick. If the floor is wood or bamboo, a solid-colored or lightly patterned quartz works well.

You have more choices than ever in today's marketplace, including old favorites such as wood and stone, and newer materials such as engineered stone, porcelain and ceramic slab, and concrete. If you start your decision-making process from the standpoint of what works for how you live, whom you live with, and what you live in, rather than which online image you loved last week, your countertop choice is more likely to serve you well in the long run.

**MIX AND MATCH.** This traditional kitchen on Florida's Gulf Coast has black-granite countertops that complement the painted white cabinets and let the warm, rich floors and festive backsplash be the stars of the room. The buffet that separates the kitchen from the butler's pantry features a walnut top that pulls its deep brown tones from the floor and helps to reinforce the traditional style of the kitchen.

**MATCHING SURFACES.** (inset) The wood counter on the kitchen's buffet closely resembles the color and tone of the wood flooring throughout the kitchen and adjoining spaces. This countertop helps connect the kitchen to the rest of the house and is a suitable material for a space that will not have to withstand the abuse of a hardworking prep space.

**CLASSIC CONTRAST.** The black-granite countertops on the working side of the kitchen are offset by white cabinets and bright-blue backsplash tiles. The tops were selected for their durability and subtleness.

# Amazing Countertops

BY ROB YAGID

**Bamboo**

**Paper**

**Solid glass**

**Recycled glass**

**Scrap metal**

Deep into a kitchen-remodeling project, I'm still undecided about what type of countertops to install. Few elements of a kitchen draw as much attention—or as much money—so I'm considering my options carefully. Like most people, I want countertops that are going to withstand years of abuse but that will still look beautiful when I'm ready to sell sometime down the road. I'm not prepared to settle on just any countertop material, though, and going against popular opinion, I'm steadfast in my aversion to granite.

Don't get me wrong. Granite and other natural stones are great countertop materials. Slabs are available nearly everywhere, they're durable, and they look great. But it seems as if everyone is putting stone counters, especially granite, in their homes these days. Granite is so prevalent that it has become, to a degree, boring. What was once a material used to achieve a distinctive, high-end style has now become expected. Solid-surface material and engineered stone don't offer much more excitement. Instead, I'm considering countertop materials that few people know about and that even fewer are using in their homes.

If you're looking for a countertop that will make a dramatic style statement instead of helping to create a kitchen that feels common, consider products made of glass, paper, bamboo, or scrap metal. Besides being durable and beautiful, many of these products promote sustainable building practices by recycling unlikely materials. They might not be the most-popular products on the market or the most-classic ones, but that's a good thing.

## Bamboo Is Renewable and Durable

It's hard not to be impressed by bamboo. The material is actually a type of grass, but it's 16-percent harder than maple. Bamboo reaches harvestable maturity in less than five years—as opposed to the 50- to 70-year growing period of hardwoods—and continuously replenishes itself by sprouting new shoots from an extensive root system. With its warm natural appearance and its ability to be easily cut and shaped with common tools, it's no wonder bamboo is being made into kitchen countertops.

**TONES AND TEXTURES CAN VARY.**
Edge-grain bamboo counters tend
to be slightly more monochromatic,
whereas other grain orientations
offer more visual texture. The darker
color of bamboo is achieved by heating the material, which caramelizes
its natural sugars.

Strips of bamboo are assembled into counters in end-grain, edge-grain, or flat-grain orientations in dimensions as large as 30 in. wide, 96 in. long, and 2 in. thick, though custom sizes are available. Bamboo can withstand a significant amount of abuse, but should be treated like any wood counter. Trivets prevent burns from hot pots and pans, and an application of penetrating sealer helps to prevent staining. Water-based polyurethane sealers tend to leave bamboo looking dull, so manufacturers recommend the use of food-safe tung oil to seal all faces of the countertop, including the bottom.

Like wood, bamboo countertops are only marginally stable. Dimensional changes occur with seasonal fluctuations in temperature and humidity. Unlike wood, bamboo shouldn't be stained because achieving an even appearance is often difficult.

A major benefit of using a bamboo countertop is that the entire length of its surface can be used as a cutting board. Any scratches or knife marks can be left or sanded away. A yearly application of proper tung oil will help to keep the countertop looking new.

**BAMBOO SOURCES**

**TOTALLY BAMBOO**
www.totallybamboo.com

**ENDURAWOOD**
www.endurawood.com

**BAMBOO REVOLUTION**
www.bamboorevolution.com

**SMITH & FONG**
www.plyboo.com

**NOT YOUR ORDINARY BUTCHER BLOCK.**
End-grain bamboo countertops conjure up
images of traditional maple butcher block.
End-grain bamboo, often referred to as
parquet, is significantly harder than maple,
making it a more-durable cutting surface.

## Paper Counters Look and Feel Like Stone

Paper might not seem like a suitable raw material for countertop fabrication, but when saturated with resin, heated, and compressed, the result is surprisingly stonelike. This type of paper-based panel is durable and has been used for years in industrial and marine applications, while also being the surface of choice for skateboard parks. Several manufacturers make these counters, but different processes result in varying performance traits.

Panels made of post-consumer waste paper are typically sought for their green attributes. This recycled paper is less uniform than virgin material, however, and can result in a countertop that varies in thickness, which can lead to installation difficulties—especially at butt joints. Virgin material, though less green, allows for tighter tolerances during fabrication.

The type of resin used to bind paper together also has an impact on the countertop. Phenolic resin, though extremely strong, is caramel in color, which limits the range of color choices. Also, UV-exposure causes phenolic resins to darken over time.

Klip Biotechnologies® has a paper-based countertop, EcoTop®, which is made with a different type of manufacturing process. Joel Klippert, the creator of EcoTop, describes the material as "a blend of bamboo fibers, which add dimensional stability to the counter; recycled demolition wood fibers; and recycled paper." These materials are bound together with a VOC-free water-based resin. The resin won't darken due to UV-exposure and is clear, which enables Klip Biotechnologies to make counters from white to black and many colors in between. Unlike other paper-based counters, EcoTop does not need to be installed by a certified technician.

All paper-based countertops can be cut and shaped with carbide-tipped blades and router bits, just like solid-surface material. Panels are available in sizes as large as 5 ft. wide, 12 ft. long, and 1¼ in. thick, depending on the manufacturer. These countertops are stain resistant, but should still be

**EASILY TOOLED, NOT EASILY DAMAGED.** Paper countertops can be cut or routed to have crisp, defined edge profiles. However, manufacturers suggest that paper counters be finished with eased edges because the material can be sharp. Cutting and shaping ease are by no means a reflection of this countertop's surprisingly strong durability.

### PAPER SOURCES

**PAPERSTONE®**
www.paperstoneproducts.com

**RICHLITE®**
www.richlite.com

**ECOTOP**
www.kliptech.com

properly finished. Some manufacturers provide their own finish product, which is a combination of natural oils and waxes that enrich the appearance of the top while protecting it from damage.

Damage that does occur, such as scratches and scorch marks, can be sanded out of the top. However, it's difficult to do without creating a blemish, so refinishing the entire top is recommended. A yearly application of mineral oil or an approved finish will help keep this top looking new.

## Solid Glass Is Modern and Easy to Clean

Glass countertops bring a clean, modern look to a kitchen. Contrary to popular perception, they are durable and are extremely sanitary because glass is nonporous and easy to clean. Glass countertops can be installed in a variety of ways, with edge treatments that range from polished to chiseled in appearance.

A glass top being fixed directly to a cabinet typically receives a coat of paint on its bottom surface prior to being secured with silicone caulk. The paint helps to hide the contents of the cabinet and gives the counter a finished look. Glass can also be installed over an opaque substrate like melamine or suspended on piers so that it appears to be floating. Stainless-steel locating pins can also be used to keep these countertops in place.

Fabricators use three types of glass to create countertops. Float glass, the material found in modern-

BEAUTY MEETS FUNCTION, AT A COST. Manufacturers can form glass into nearly any shape, texture, and color. This allows their tops to have great visual appeal while masking fingerprints and scratches. Similar to most other art, the more elaborate the piece (below), the higher the price tag.

day windowpanes, can be used to make counters as large as roughly 6 ft. wide, 10 ft. long, and ¾ in. thick. Manufacturers often temper this glass to improve its strength and safety in the unlikely event that it breaks.

Slump glass is distinguished by its shapes and textures. Slump glass is simply float glass that is placed on top of a carved mold, then heated so that the glass relaxes and "slumps" into the contours of the mold.

Kiln-fired glass, also known as cast glass or art glass, is made of recycled glass fragments that have been placed in a kiln and heated until they bond

back together. Kiln-fired glass is as strong as the other types of glass, if not stronger. Thick glass countertops are most often made of kiln-fired glass, which can be more than 2 in. thick. Kiln-fired tops can be made only as large as the kiln that fabricators have access to, typically 6 ft. wide by 12 ft. long.

Glass-countertop fabricators are split in their recommendations for where their products can or should be used. "Glass counters shouldn't be used anywhere they'll receive a significant amount of abuse," says Jim Duncan of Duncan Glass. Along with some other manufacturers, Duncan thinks that glass tops should be reserved for non-utility areas in the kitchen, such as accent pieces or island tops. Others say that glass performs like natural stone and can be used safely as a work surface. Fabricators agree on one point, however: Glass scratches. Although scratches and fingerprints are less noticeable on a textured or colored top, repair or replacement of a glass counter can be expensive.

Glass tops have few maintenance requirements. Just clean them with a nonabrasive product like Windex®.

## Recycled-Glass Counters Are Now Easier to Find

Although countertops made of cement and recycled glass have been around for more than a decade, production has been low and manufacturers have been scarce. These days, more and more companies

# MAKING CONCRETE COUNTERS IS EASIER THAN EVER

**BECAUSE THEY ARE CRAFTED BY HAND**, no two concrete countertops are ever exactly alike, resulting in a top that evokes a true artisanal feel. Although the number of concrete-countertop specialists has continued to grow, so too have the resources for first-time fabricators.

Manufacturers like Cheng Design and Buddy Rhodes now provide all the materials needed to design and fabricate concrete countertops. They sell specially blended concrete mixes, pigments, sealers, and sink molds. Instructional videos and books are also available. They even host instructional workshops around the country.

If you've been having trouble finding a durable countertop that has true custom appeal, there has never been a better time to build it yourself. (For more information on building your own, see "A New Approach to Concrete Countertops" on pp. 204–211.)

### CONCRETE SOURCES

**BUDDY RHODES**
www.buddyrhodes.com

**CHENG DESIGN**
www.chengdesign.com

To locate other fabricators and suppliers, visit www.concretenetwork.com.

are salvaging glass fragments, which are available in countless colors and shapes, and mixing them with cement or epoxy resin to make countertops. Recycled glass is a major component of each mix, making up roughly 75 percent to 85 percent of the finished countertop, depending on the manufacturer.

Fabricators shape and install these countertops like natural stone, with a similar selection of edge profiles. Sizes as large as 9 ft. by 5 ft. are available. Leaving a hot pot on the surface won't result in burn marks on a recycled-glass countertop, but it could affect the top's sealer. For this reason, trivets are recommended.

Recycled-glass counters constructed with a cement binder are slightly different than those made with epoxy resin. Cement can be stained by acids in wine, vinegar, and citrus juices, so these countertops need to be sealed, maintained, and cleaned of spills with more diligence than counters made with resin. Resin, however, is not as hard as a cement-based surface and always requires the use of trivets and cutting boards.

Most cement counters come sealed but require re-sealing every couple of years with an impregnating sealer. Resin-based counters don't need sealing but should be polished with a paste wax to maintain their finish.

**FROM THE CURB TO THE KITCHEN.** When bottles and windows are broken, windshields fractured, and traffic lights decommissioned, some of this glass is recycled, and a lot of it ends up in the landfill. More and more of it, however, is being used to make unique, durable countertops.

## RECYCLED-GLASS SOURCES

**VETRAZZO**
www.vetrazzo.com

**ICESTONE®**
www.icestoneusa.com

**TIGER MOUNTAIN INNOVATIONS**
www.trinityglassproducts.com

**ENVIROGLAS®**
www.enviroglasproducts.com

UNIFORM EDGES ARE MORE CONVINCING.
By eliminating the seam at a laminate top's
edges, manufacturers like VT Industries can
create counters that are more-easily passed
off as solid-slab material.

## Laminate Never Looked so Good

Created in 1914 for use as an electric insulator, plastic laminate has long proven itself as a highly durable material. It wasn't until many years after its creation, though, that people realized it would make an excellent countertop surface. Laminate is non-porous, stain resistant, and warm to the touch. It also absorbs impact (which leads to fewer broken glasses) and requires little maintenance. When laminate is bypassed as a countertop material, it's often because of a style threshold defined by shiny surfaces and poor imitations of stone and wood.

Modern laminates, though, are better than they have ever been, thanks to higher-quality decorative layers, newly developed textured surfaces, and refined edge details that eliminate the telltale seam that marks laminate transitions. Just about anyone with basic carpentry skills can fabricate laminate counters, and with today's products, they can create countertops that look anything but plastic.

## Scrap-Metal Countertops Save Resources

As the green-building trend continues to grow, products made from recycled materials are becoming more popular. Of the nearly 3 million tons of aluminum that are discarded every year in the United States, a small portion is being used to create countertops that can set your kitchen apart.

### LAMINATE SOURCES

**WILSONART**
www.wilsonart.com

**FORMICA**
www.formica.com

**PIONITE®**
www.pionite.com

**VT INDUSTRIES**
www.vtindustries.com

Available through dealers and fabricators nationwide, Alkemi countertops are made by mixing aluminum shavings with UV-stable polymeric resin. The countertop material contains at least 60 percent post-industrial scrap aluminum, which conventional recyclers don't use. Installed over a plywood substrate with silicone caulk, these counters are easily worked by carbide-tipped tools and are maintained like ordinary solid-surface materials.

Eleek Inc. of Portland, Oregon, fabricates solid ¼-in.-thick countertops and tiles made of recycled aluminum that has been cast in reusable silicone molds. The products are an environmentally friendly

POLISHED OR HONED, BUT ALWAYS MADE WITH ALUMINUM. Alkemi uses only aluminum shavings in its countertops. The variety of colored shavings, like bronze or copper, is acquired by anodizing the shavings prior to mixing them with resin. Alkemi tops are available with either a smooth, honed surface (above left) or a textured surface (above right).

alternative to metal countertops such as stainless steel, zinc, and pewter, and still have an easy-to-maintain, industrial aesthetic. Each countertop is custom-built and available with an integrated rolled front edge and backsplash, so further on-site fabrication is not needed. Eleek's countertops and tiles are installed with mastic when placed over cement board or construction adhesive when applied to a plywood substrate. Eleek's products come with one caveat. They can't be cut on site without compromising the powder-coated finish. This places a much larger emphasis on precise templating and layouts prior to ordering.

## SCRAP-METAL SOURCES

**ALKEMI**
www.renewedmaterials.com

**ELEEK INC.**
www.eleekinc.com

ARTISTIC FINISHES HELP TO CREATE NATURAL SURFACES. Eleek countertops and tiles can be powder coated in a variety of colors or given a natural-looking patina by an in-house artisan. Their patina finishes help to convey truly custom work, and no two products look exactly the same.

# METAL COUNTERTOP OPTIONS

**BY NENA DONOVAN LEVINE**

The popularity of metal-countertop materials has grown considerably over the years. All of them offer homeowner-friendly benefits. They're all easy to keep clean and are relatively resilient when treated with care. However, none are inexpensive, and metal prices fluctuate so often that speaking in generalities is more accurate than giving definitive numbers. Here's what distinguishes each material.

## A STAINLESS STEEL

An alloy of carbon steel, nickel, and chromium, stainless steel doesn't oxidize or develop a patina like other metals, so it has a consistent look throughout its service time. Although stainless doesn't have the antimicrobial benefits of some other metals, it is less porous, which means it's easy to keep clean. Stainless steel is classified into "series" based on the percentage of each component element, and it is further classified into "grades" based on its crystalline structure. Countertops most often are made of grade-304 stainless, the hardest of the materials discussed here and the most scratch resistant.

**Finishes:**
Stainless-steel finishes are numbered from 0 to 8 based on their polish; the higher the number, the shinier the surface. However, a brushed finish is most popular for countertops because it shows less wear and fewer fingerprints than a mirror finish.

**Cost ranking:** Lowest

## B ZINC

Zinc is a discrete element, whereas stainless steel, pewter, and bronze are alloys. An ordinary gray color, zinc is known (if at all) as a countertop material for oyster and seafood bars in Europe. Seams are welded and should be ground flush, but they are often visible due to color variations among zinc sheets. A good designer or fabricator can suggest a design compatible with the maximum sheet size, which is usually around 120 in. by 39 in. Zinc is not as hard as other metals, so it should be cleaned with a nonabrasive cleanser, and trivets should be used whenever possible to prevent damage.

**Finishes:**
Zinc counters can be polished to a mirror sheen, but that's like polishing your work boots. The natural finish will develop a patina, or oxidation on the metal's surface. Applying beeswax can help to keep the countertop looking new.

**Cost ranking:** Low

## C PEWTER

Pewter, an alloy that is mostly tin, resembles zinc in that it is naturally gray in appearance. When pewter develops a patina, it becomes a deep gray. Like zinc, pewter counters can create a distinctly European style as their use is more prevalent there. Pewter is the softest of these metals and melts so easily that it must be soldered, not welded. It is not as resilient as other metal countertops, but its softness is suited to intricately worked edge treatments. Like other soft metals, pewter should be treated with extreme care. Abrasive cleaners will scratch it, and a hardworking kitchen will take its toll.

**Finishes:**
The results of aging are the same as zinc. Pewter countertops should also be maintained with beeswax.

**Cost ranking:** Highest

A

B

C

D

E

Zinc with an
aged finish

Pewter with an
aged finish

Copper with an
aged finish

Bronze with an
aged finish

### D COPPER

According to the U.S. Geological Survey, copper ranks as the third most widely consumed metal on earth and one of the first metals used by man. When used in the kitchen, it can provide both an industrial and an old-world look. Like other metals, copper develops a patina over time, and its bright luster dulls as it ages. More so than other metals, copper has an inherent antimicrobial quality, which makes it a hygienic countertop option. Copper is relatively soft and malleable, so it should be treated with care to prevent damage.

**Finishes:**
Copper can be polished to a high shine, left untreated so that it develops a patina, or chemically "aged" and sealed. Its finish can be maintained with copper cleaner and with waxes such as Trewax®.

**Cost ranking: Moderate**

### E BRONZE

Bronze is a metal alloy primarily composed of copper and tin, but it can contain other elements. It develops a patina over time, turning a dark, golden-brown color. Only a stainless-steel countertop is harder than bronze. However, bronze can still be scratched; as with all other metal countertops, cutting boards should be used. Bronze can be cleaned with a nonabrasive cleanser.

**Finishes:**
The options are the same as zinc, pewter, and copper. Bronze countertops are often appealing to those who like the look of copper but find its hue too jarring. The finish can be maintained with the same products used for copper.

**Cost ranking: High**

### WHY NOT ALUMINUM?

Inexpensive and readily available, aluminum seems like a great countertop option. So why, then, does aluminum seem to be the least popular metal among manufacturers and fabricators?

Aluminum is much softer than stainless steel but is still relatively resilient. The material has a few major drawbacks, though. Aluminum that is not treated with a protective finish, like a powder or clear coating, can stain and oxidize when it comes in contact with water and other substances found in kitchens. Unlike other metals, oxidized aluminum has a white, crusty appearance. It doesn't look patinated or well aged; it just looks unattractive.

Aluminum can be bent easily, but fabricating the metal into a countertop can be very difficult. Welding aluminum is extremely hard, especially when working with the thin 16-ga. metal that most countertops are made of. Aluminum's susceptibility to warping under extreme heat is heightened by the process.

# STILL INTERESTED IN STONE?

**BY JENNIFER STIMPSON**

**IF YOU STILL HAVE YOUR HEART SET ON A STONE COUNTERTOP** you'll need to take into consideration its care. It's a common misconception that applying sealer to a stone countertop is all that's needed to protect it from damage. Unfortunately, even after sealer is applied, stone is susceptible to scratches, staining, chipping, and heat damage. Knowing the compositional qualities of each stone is the best way to choose a countertop that can handle the wear and tear of a busy kitchen.

## A LIMESTONE

**Profile:**
Certain types of limestone, such as the popular Jerusalem gold, are very dense and very durable. However, most other limestone is soft and easily damaged, even more so than marble.

**Surface notes:**
Limestone that is not dense isn't recommended for use in busy kitchens. Its high porosity and susceptibility to damage can show after only a couple of years of heavy use.

**Finishes:** Honed or polished

## B MARBLE

**Profile:**
Marble is a very soft stone, so it cannot withstand high heat, and it is easily etched by acidic substances such as orange juice.

**Surface notes:**
Marble is known for its natural ability to stay cool and is often preferred by professional chefs for rolling dough and making pastries. The patina of polished or aged marble is prized for its traditional, old-world appeal. When selecting marble counters, remember that a polished finish makes surface imperfections more noticeable, whereas a honed or brushed finish helps to mask any scratches.

**Finishes:** Polished, honed, or brushed

### E SOAPSTONE

**Profile:**
Soapstone is dense and soft, and it is the least-porous stone-countertop material available. It is often used in science laboratories that demand clean, sterile environments, which isn't much different than the demands of a kitchen.

**Surface notes:**
Because soapstone is impenetrable, it is resistant to stains, bacteria growth, and damage from acidic substances. Soapstone comes in three colors: gray, green, and black. Similar to slate, soapstone's color might not be fully realized until a weekly application of mineral oil has taken place for nearly a year.

**Finish:** Honed

### D GRANITE

**Profile:**
Granite is one of the hardest stones and is virtually scratch resistant. A low porosity and a very high heat resistance make it a popular countertop material for active kitchens.

**Surface notes:**
Granite is less porous than other stone but still needs to be sealed to reduce its porosity. If you're sealing granite with an impregnating sealer, be sure to do it every six months. If the slab was sealed professionally by the manufacturer, it might not require resealing for up to five years.

**Finishes:** Honed, polished, flamed, sandblasted, or brushed

### C SLATE

**Profile:**
High-quality, dense slate is less absorbent and more durable than many countertop materials, so it doesn't require sealing like other types of stone countertops.

**Surface notes:**
Due to its low porosity, slate is less likely to harbor bacteria. However, its uneven surface makes slate counters difficult to clean. Slate should be periodically treated with mineral oil to reduce its chalky appearance and to enhance its color tone.

**Finishes:** Honed, polished, or cleft

# Cut a Laminate Countertop for a Sink

BY ANDY ENGEL

When you're building or remodeling a kitchen you can save time and money by using a ready-made laminate countertop. These tops, which generally have an integral backsplash and wraparound front edge, are durable and easy to find at home centers and lumberyards. Even if you have a laminate top custom-fabricated or you make it yourself, you can still use the sink-cutting methods described here.

Many sinks come with a layout template that makes marking the cut easy; you just trace the template with a pencil and cut out the hole with a jigsaw. If you don't have a template, trace around the sink rim with a pencil, and then adjust the line inward to get the proper fit. On dark tops like this one, I make the layout marks on light-colored masking tape so they're easier to see.

I cut most of the opening with a jigsaw equipped with a laminate-cutting blade. These blades cut on the downstroke to prevent chipping. If the countertop has an integral backsplash, there's usually not enough room for a jigsaw when making the rear cut (adjacent to the backsplash). I make this cut with an oscillating multitool.

After making the rear cut, I attach a cleat to the cutout with a single screw. The cleat supports the cutout in place to prevent the countertop from breaking as the cut is finished. I use one screw so I can rotate the cleat out of the blade's path while cutting.

To make less mess, you might be tempted to cut the top outdoors or in your shop and then move the prepared top to the sink base. I generally don't do this, because with a large hole in the center it's very easy to break the countertop while moving it.

**CENTER THE SINK.** Use a combination square lined up between the cabinet doors to establish the side-to-side location of the sink. Make sure the front cut won't hit the cabinet rail below.

**TRACE THE LINE.** Trace the template or the sink rim as the starting point for layout lines. A layer of tape helps you see the pencil lines.

**MOVE THE LINE INWARD.** Without a template, the layout line must be moved inward so it will be covered by the sink rim. The margins vary by sink, but the minimum is about ¼ in. Make a mark at both ends of all four sides.

**CONNECT THE DOTS.** (left) Use a straightedge to connect the marks that correspond with the actual cutline. (inset) Connect the corners at an angle for an easier cut and better sink support.

**DOUBLE-CHECK THE LAYOUT.** Confirm that the cuts will be covered fully by the sink rim, then cross out the original lines to prevent cutting on the wrong line.

# MAKE THE CUT

To prevent damaging the laminate countertop, use a reverse-cutting jigsaw blade. These blades have teeth that cut on the downstroke instead of the upstroke. Go slowly, and apply steady downward pressure so that the saw doesn't bounce while cutting.

There's often not enough room to fit a jigsaw between the back of the sink and the backsplash. In these instances, use a fine-tooth blade in an oscillating multitool. Make the cut in several passes so you don't overheat the blade, which slows cutting and dulls the teeth.

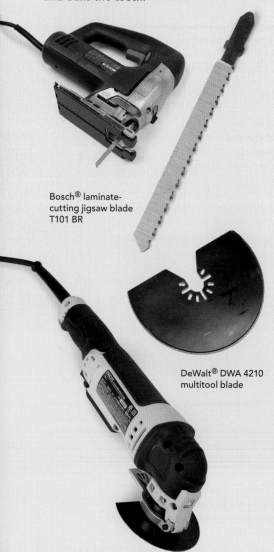

Bosch® laminate-cutting jigsaw blade T101 BR

DeWalt® DWA 4210 multitool blade

**DRILL THE CORNERS.** Drill the insides of every corner with a ⅜-in. spade bit. Make sure the holes are fully within the lines that mark the actual sink cutout.

**CUT THE BACK.** Because of the backsplash, there's generally not enough room to cut the back side with a jigsaw. Instead, use a fine-tooth blade in an oscillating multitool.

**ATTACH A CLEAT.** To prevent the top from breaking as you finish the cut, secure a cleat to the top. A single screw in the center allows you to rotate the cleat out of the way while cutting.

**FINISH UP WITH A JIGSAW.** Use a jigsaw with a reverse-cutting blade to finish the sink cutout. Maintain downward pressure to keep the saw from bouncing as it cuts.

**TEST THE FIT.** After checking that the sink fits inside the cutout, clean all dust from the countertop, run a bead of silicone sealant around the rim, and install the clips that secure the sink.

# Tiling Over a Laminate Counter

BY DAVID HART

I tear out tons of tub surrounds and sheet vinyl every year and install ceramic tile. That type of remodeling makes up the bulk of my work. Other than an occasional mud-set floor, I use cementitious backerboard as tile underlayment on walls and floors. After having mixed results with plywood, I found that backerboard also works great for countertop renovations.

The major advantage to installing backerboard over an existing laminate countertop is that it keeps down the total cost of the tile installation. Instead of building a new countertop, I set the tile on a sheet of ¼ -in. backerboard that's screwed to the old laminate. The backerboard provides a sturdy, stable substrate for the tile, it saves me a day (or more) of labor, and it can knock several hundred dollars off the total cost of the project. (Obviously, this method won't work on postformed counters.)

Why not install the tile directly on the countertop? It doesn't work. I learned the hard way that latex- or polymer-modified thinsets don't bond well to plastic laminate, even though a mortar manufacturer assured me that they would. After two installation failures involving only thinset, I now overlay the laminate with backerboard and haven't had a callback since.

## Make Sure the Original Counter Is Sound

Because a new sink is often part of a counter renovation, my first step is to determine the size of the new sink cutout. If the new sink is smaller than the original, I have to rebuild the counter to give the sink proper support before overlaying the top with backerboard. If the new sink dimensions are larger,

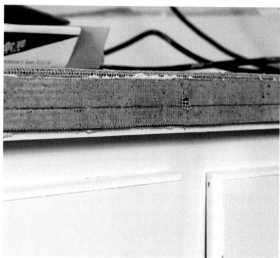

CUT THE BACKERBOARD. (left) Cutting backerboard with a grinder is dusty but quick. Although backerboard can be scored with a utility knife and snapped, an angle grinder fitted with a diamond blade cuts a cleaner line faster.

NARROWER EDGE STRIPS ARE MORE EASILY CONCEALED. (below) To ensure that the tile covers the backerboard, the author keeps the edge strips at least ¼ in. back from the counter's edge.

I cut the countertop to the correct size and continue with the installation. (It's also worth noting here that unless they have flexible water supplies, most sinks need to be replumbed due to the increased depth of the counter.)

I also check the condition of the counter's particleboard. Prolonged exposure to steam from a dishwasher or water seepage from around the sink can turn particleboard into little more than loose sawdust. The best way to check is to crawl into the base cabinet and examine the underside of the countertop with a flashlight. If I can dig particleboard apart with a screwdriver or pocketknife, or if it's swelling from exposure to moisture, then the damage is probably too severe to use this installation method. Scrap the existing top, rebuild it, and quit reading this chapter.

All laminate countertops will move when you pound a fist on them, but excessive movement will lead to cracked grout joints and, eventually, loose tiles. Cement backerboards help to tighten any floor or countertop if installed properly, but bouncy or spongy tops need to be fixed or scrapped. Often, a few screws driven up into the countertop through the cabinets' corner brackets will stiffen a bouncy top.

It's also important at this early stage to measure the height of the tiles that cover the edge of the counter (called V-cap) and compare that dimension to the height of the countertop's finished edge. The V-cap should cover the countertop edge and backerboard. Typical V-cap covers about 1¾ in., which doesn't leave much tile hanging below the substrate; some run deeper, and others run a little shallower. I also make sure the cabinet drawers don't hit the tile overhang.

**AN AUTOFEED SCREW GUN SPEEDS A TEDIOUS JOB.** (above) Faced with a day of driving screws into substrate, the author uses an autofeed screw gun that starts and seats each screw much faster than by hand.

**THINSET INCREASES THE BOND.** (left) Like peanut butter spread between two pieces of bread, thinset troweled onto the counter will fill voids beneath the backerboard and strengthen the substrate.

## Cutting Cement Backerboard

If I need to keep the job site clean, sometimes I cut backerboard with a utility knife and a straightedge. Although it's slightly more expensive than other backerboard, Durock® is somewhat softer and easier to cut with a standard utility knife. Yes, I burn through blades, but it's quick and virtually dust-free.

Utility knives don't work well on harder, slicker boards such as Wonderboard, so to cut those types of board I rely on a right-angle grinder with 4-in. dry-cut diamond blade. A vital piece of equipment for compound or circular cuts as well, this tool throws a cloud of dust anytime I cut cement board with it, so I never use it in an enclosed space.

I always lay the board in place dry to check the fit; I usually allow up to a ½-in. gap between the counter and wall and up to a ¼-in. gap between individual pieces of board. The important thing here is that I don't want the backerboard to extend beyond the edges of the top. After I cut the backerboard to fit the existing top, I cut strips for the counter's edge about ¼ in. narrower than the edge of the countertop so that the backerboard doesn't stick out below the bottom of the edge cap.

## Modified Thinset and Screws Make a Better Bond

By itself, ¼-in. backerboard offers no additional strength when attached directly to the substrate; a layer of thinset beneath the backerboard fills the voids and creates a vacuum that is nearly impossible to break. I never skip this step. Unmodified mortar doesn't provide any bond to the laminate, although it will stick to the backerboard, so I always spend the few extra dollars and get latex or polymer-modified thinset, which cures harder than unmodified mortar and allows a small amount of deflection.

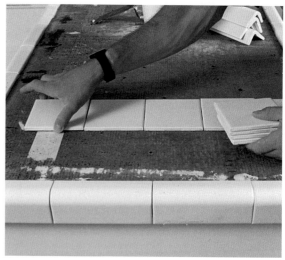

**LAYOUT STARTS FROM THE CENTER.** (above) To ensure a well-spaced layout, the author places whole tiles across the space, using a center mark as a reference. The remaining space is divided into two partial tiles.

**V-CAPS GO ON FIRST.** (left) These narrow right-angle tiles form a border for the square field tiles. Starting at the exterior bullnose corners, the V-caps are laid out in an equal pattern that ends at a wall or a mitered inside corner.

It's important to mix thinset with the proper amount of water. As a rule, too much water will create a weak bond; too little makes the product tough to trowel, and it may not bond to the tile or backerboard properly. I try to mix it so that it has a smooth, creamy consistency. If the mix clings to my trowel without running off and still spreads easily, then I know I've got a good mix.

After mixing a batch of thinset, I trowel it onto the counter with a ¼-in. notch trowel, trying not to spread more thinset than I can use in ten or fifteen minutes. For an experienced tilesetter, that can mean the entire counter, but for those new to this type of work, that might mean covering a small section at one time. Once a section of counter is covered, I lay the backerboard in place and screw it down.

Because the board is only ¼ in. thick, I use screws that are 1 in. long. Longer screws might protrude

through the bottom of the particleboard and give someone a nasty scrape. I like to space the screws about 6 in. apart on the perimeter of the board and 8 in. to 10 in. apart on the inside. Although I have used loose screws and a screw gun, I usually rely on a Makita® autofeed screw gun; it's just quicker. I try to make sure that there are no bubbles in the backerboard and that I seat the screw heads flush or slightly below the surface.

## Tile Layout: Big Tiles Are Better

Once the counter is ready, I take time for a careful tile layout. Nothing will ruin an installation more than a poor layout. For this project I first installed the 6-in. V-caps, starting from the outside corners and working toward the wall. I butter the backside of each tile as I go, which makes the next step cleaner. Once the edge is complete, I lay out the interior tile

**GROUT WORKS BEST WHEN SPREAD IN SMALL AREAS.** Worked into tile joints with a rubber float, grout tends to set up quickly, and it becomes difficult to remove from the tile surface. A clean, damp sponge is the best tool to wipe excess grout from tiles and to smooth grout lines.

pattern dry to see which tiles will have to be cut. On a perfect installation, I would end up with full tiles across the full width of the counter, but that never happens. The best installation will have the largest tiles possible in the most visible areas. And I'll often try to cut a small amount from tiles on both sides of the layout rather than cutting a large amount from the tiles on one side.

Once I've checked the layout, I start applying enough thinset to keep me going for about ten minutes. If the mix sits on the backerboard for much longer than that, it starts to skim over, and then it won't bond with the tile.

## Apply Small Areas of Grout

After the tile is set, I wait a day for the thinset to cure before I start grouting. Most grout has a modifier in it, which creates a stronger, more stain-resistant grout, so there's no need to add latex to the dry powder. The grout/water mix should be stiffer than toothpaste, but loose enough to push across the tile without great force.

Using a rubber float, I usually won't spread more grout than I can work in about ten minutes. I don't allow the grout to sit on the tile surface for long, either; once it has hardened, the grout is difficult to remove. I use a large damp sponge to smooth the joints and to wipe off the face of the tile. It's important not to wipe too much out of the joints, to rinse the sponge frequently, and to wring the excess water out of the sponge. Too much water can discolor or weaken grout.

# Tiling a Backsplash

BY TOM MEEHAN

Saturday is estimate day at our store, Cape Cod Tileworks. Of the five or six estimates we do on Saturday mornings, at least a third of them are for kitchen backsplashes. Whether the room is new or old, a backsplash is a great opportunity to express a kitchen's qualities, including color, creativity, boldness, subtlety, and craftsmanship. If you haven't done a lot of tiling, a backsplash is a great way to get your feet wet.

## Layout: A Road Map for the Backsplash

Once the tile has been selected, the next step is layout. For this project, my client chose tumbled-marble tile. Its coarse natural texture makes a particularly nice contrast to a smooth, shiny kitchen countertop, such as granite.

The layout for most of this backsplash is fairly simple: three courses of 4-in. by 4-in. tile topped off

by a narrow border; a filler course takes care of the space between the border and the wall cabinets. The challenging part is the patterned area behind the stove. Taller and more intricate than the rest of the backsplash, this area requires a layout that is dead-on accurate (see the photos below). My first step is measuring the exact dimensions of that space.

Over the years, I've found that doing the layout directly on the wall doesn't work well. Instead, I draw a full-size layout of the patterned area on a sheet of cardboard. Then I cut and arrange all the tiles as needed to fit the layout. I don't start to set tile on the wall until the test-fit is complete. This backsplash features small square dots at the intersections of the diamonds. At this point, I mark and cut these types of elements as well.

If a backsplash is interrupted by a window, it looks best if the tiles on each side of the window are the same size, which often means using partial tiles elsewhere. I plan the size and location of these partial tiles to please the eye.

Electrical outlets have to be incorporated into most backsplashes. A symmetrical layout around an electrical box looks best and is the easiest to cut. In extreme cases, the box can be moved for a proper-looking layout.

**TEST-FIT THE TILES ON A FLAT SURFACE.** For the area above the stove, the author first measures the exact dimensions (top left photo). Decorative elements such as the border and the square accent tiles are cut and fit (bottom left photo). Then he transfers them to a sheet of cardboard, where all the tile is dry-fit (right photo).

**TROWEL ON THE MASTIC.** White mastic is the adhesive of choice for this project because a darker color might show through the light-colored tile. The entire backsplash is spread before any tile is set.

## Install the Tile in the Right Order

Before mud and mastic start flying, it's critical to protect appliances, countertops, and other finished surfaces. For this installation, a rubber shower-pan liner and a piece of cardboard protect the countertop and floors. The rubber liner is great because it can take a little impact if something is dropped on it. It also stays put, unlike a plastic drop cloth.

When I'm ready to set tile, I spread all-purpose mastic on the wall using a trowel with ¼-in. by ¼-in. notches (see the photo above). Because the tumbled marble for this backsplash is a fairly light color, I used nonstaining white mastic, which prevents the tile from spotting or darkening.

I set the bottom course of tiles for the backsplash first, after putting spacers under the tiles to keep them ⅛ in. above the counter. If the counter has to be replaced in the future, this space provides enough room to slip in the new countertop without disturbing the backsplash.

To install each tile, I press it tightly against the wall about ¼ in. from its final position, then slide it in place to ensure a tight bond. With the bottom course in place, I turn to the trickiest part of the job, the patterned area behind the stove. Border pieces go in first (see the photos on the facing page). To create visual interest, I like the border to stand slightly proud of surrounding tiles, a subtle strategy that's not difficult to do. Before installing each border piece, I butter the back with mastic. When the tile is pressed in place, the extra mastic makes the border stand out slightly from the rest of the tile. Setting a few of the regular backsplash tiles outside the border helps keep the border pieces straight.

As I place tiles, I make the grout joints roughly ¼ in. wide. Because these tiles are irregular, the joint

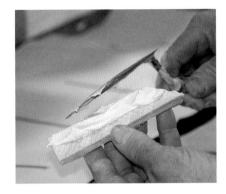

**START AT THE BORDER.** To make the border tiles stand slightly proud of the rest of the tile, the backs receive a coat of mastic first (top left). This will cause the tiles to stand out from the rest of the field when they're pressed into place (bottom left). To install a tile, press it against the wall and slide it about ¼ in. into position. Align diamond-shaped tiles along their long edges (right).

size varies somewhat. Instead of relying on spacers, I shift the tiles slightly as the different sizes require.

For the diamond pattern of the backsplash, I install the tiles in a diagonal sequence to keep them aligned along their longest straight edge. The tiny square accent pieces go in as I set the larger diamond tiles.

Once the stove backsplash is done, the rest of the job goes quickly. The main backsplash is only four courses high, and it's fairly easy to keep the grout lines level and straight.

As for the cut tiles that fit against the end walls and upper cabinets, I cut them for a tight fit with little or no grout joint. Grout is most likely to crack where different materials meet.

## Seal the Tile before Grouting

I leave the tile overnight to let the mastic set up. The next day, I wipe down the backsplash with a

good impregnator/sealer, which helps protect the marble and acts as a grout release. Grouting tumbled-marble tile is a little more difficult than grouting standard glazed tile. Grout tends to catch and collect along the irregular edges and on the surface of tumbled marble as well as in the relief of the border tiles.

I always use sanded grout with tumbled marble. Sand mixes with portland cement to add body and strength to the grout, making it superior at filling the wide joints between irregular tile edges. Border tiles such as the ones in this project also demand a stronger grout because they sit farther out than the rest of the tile.

I mix a stiff but workable batch of grout that won't fall out of the joints as I float it on in a generous coat. When all the joints are filled, I let the grout sit until it is firm to the touch, usually 15 minutes or so. Then

# WORKING AROUND AN ELECTRICAL OUTLET

**SYMMETRICAL COVERAGE LOOKS BEST** when tile meets an electrical box. Mark the edges of the box on surrounding tiles and cut them to fit (see the top photo below). Cut the tile so that the ears on the outlets and the switches overlap the edges of the tile. Before installing the tiles around the box, back out the screws that secure the outlets and switches. Longer screws may be necessary to make up for the added thickness of the tile (see the bottom photo below).

I wipe the tile with a grout sponge dampened with clean water. I make sure to wring out the sponge before wiping the tile; too much water can dissolve the cement and weaken the grout. When cleaning marble tiles, I pay extra attention to rough spots in the marble and to the patterned areas in the border tiles. These areas may need a little more effort to remove excess grout.

After washing it, I let the grout set up for another 15 minutes (less, if the room is warmer than normal). Then I use a clean terry-cloth towel to wipe the grout haze off the tile surface. At this point, I also use a putty knife to remove any grout stuck in corners or in other places where I want to see a clean, straight grout line.

The next day, I do a final cleaning with a good tile cleaner. Because some cleaners corrode or stain, I keep the countertop, stove, and sink protected. A day or two after cleaning, I finish the job by applying sealer to the tile and grout. If the tile is stone (as in this case) and I sealed the tile before grouting, an additional coat of sealer also protects the grout. I apply the sealer with a disposable foam brush and give the backsplash behind the stove a couple of extra coats to protect the tile and grout from grease.

SEAL. GROUT. SEAL AGAIN. Stone tile should be sealed before grouting to prevent the grout from sticking to it (above). After grout is applied (right) and becomes firm, remove the excess with a sponge and dry cloth.

WHEN THE GROUT HAS CURED FOR 48 HOURS, a final coat of sealer provides additional protection for the tile and the grout.

# Make Your Own Laminate Countertops

BY STEVE MORRIS

Choosing a kitchen countertop is a big deal. The surface has to be durable, attractive, and complementary to the kitchen's style. The decision becomes more difficult when you consider cost. You can spend thousands of dollars on the countertops for an average kitchen, but you don't have to. Fabricating and installing a laminate countertop can save you loads of money.

The popularity of expensive countertop materials like granite, solid surface, and engineered stone makes it easy to overlook the appeal of plastic laminate. But laminate countertops still have the durability and beauty to compete with more expensive options, and there are more colors and patterns to choose from than with any other material.

Making your own laminate countertops doesn't require many tools, and the price of materials—laminate, particleboard, and contact cement—is insignificant. You can make countertops in a garage or in a basement, or you can work outside if the weather is nice.

## Start with a Custom Fit

One benefit of laminate countertops is that they can be made to fit large, oddly shaped areas without seams. Sheets of laminate are available as large as 5 ft. by 12 ft. But before I get to the laminate, I have

**THE SUBSTRATE IS CRITICAL.** To ensure accuracy, the author fabricates the substrate where it will be installed. Here, he's truing a particleboard edge by guiding a router against a straightedge.

to build a substrate. The substrate is the structural part of the countertop to which the laminate is glued. Whether I am fabricating a large, oddly shaped kitchen countertop or a small bathroom-vanity top, I prefer to prepare the substrate in place—right in the kitchen, in this case. This way, I can be sure the finished countertop will fit correctly.

Particleboard is the best material to use for the substrate, and fortunately it is the least expensive. Plywood is too grainy, and medium-density fiberboard (MDF) is too heavy. Particleboard is strong enough to do the job and provides a smooth surface for laminate. I use $^{11}/_{16}$-in. particleboard to make my countertops.

If the kitchen is large enough to set up sawhorses and if the room can be sealed to contain dust, I work right in the kitchen. Otherwise, I set up outside. I measure from the walls to the edges of the cabinet frames and add ¾ in. Later, when I add wood strips to the edges, the overhang will increase to 1½ in. If the cabinets have full-overlay doors and drawer fronts, the result will be a finished overhang of ¾ in. (see the drawing on p. 192).

## ENDLESS CHOICES AND UNBEATABLE PRICES

**THESE DAYS, EVERYONE WANTS KITCHENS** full of granite and stainless steel because they are durable and attractive. But before you write off laminate as a choice for your kitchen countertops, consider this: Among only a few major laminate suppliers, there are hundreds of styles and colors to choose from. From the look of stone, metal, and glass to wood-grain patterns and solid colors, there is a style and color to complement any kitchen or bathroom. Laminate is available in different grades, including fire-rated, chemical-resistant, and abrasion-resistant materials. Laminate is durable and easy to work with. The edges take a number of interesting treatments, including simple bevels and wood nosings. And laminate costs as little as a few dollars per sq. ft. Add the cost of the substrate, the glue, and your time, and laminate countertops still cost a fraction of the alternatives.

Laminated edges have the look of solid-surface material.

Wood nosing can be made to match the cabinets.

A half-round nosing softens the countertop edge.

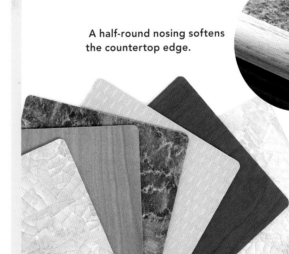

**PREPARING THE SUBSTRATE.** Walls can be bowed, and corners aren't always square. If you measure, mark, and cut the particleboard substrate in place, you can make sure that the countertop fits the cabinets and the walls.

**SCRIBE NOW, NOT LATER.** The substrate should fit flush against the wall, and the overhang should be consistent along the length of the cabinets. Scribe and cut the particleboard to fit the walls now to avoid having to cut the finished countertop during installation.

I cut the particleboard with a circular saw guided by a straightedge. Then I put the substrate in place to make sure it fits well. This often means scribing the particleboard to the walls. It is safer to cut the scribes on the blank substrate than to cut the laminated top during installation.

I avoid joining sheets of particleboard when I can. Sometimes, however, joints are inevitable. Preparing the substrate in place allows me to determine the best spots for joints. Even with thorough filing and sanding, particleboard joints can show up in finished countertops. For this reason, I try to hide the joints in corners or under the top cabinets.

Particleboard sheets are joined with biscuits and countertop bolts. On a 2-ft. joint, I use four biscuits and two bolts. The T-shaped mortises for the bolts are cut freehand with a router and a 1/2-in. straight bit. The biscuits help with surface alignment, and the bolts pull the joint together. I then file and sand the top of the joint to make sure it is smooth.

## Build a Stronger Countertop

To provide strength and to make the countertop look 1 1/2 in. thick, I reinforce the edges with 3-in.-wide strips of particleboard. Along the front and along any exposed edges, the strips are glued and nailed flush and are sanded smooth with a belt sander. In the back, where the countertop meets the walls, the strips are recessed about 1/4 in. Any area at which the countertop overhangs the cabinets by more than 6 in., such as a bar top, is doubled up entirely.

Attaching 3/4-in. by 1 1/2-in. hardwood strips to the front edge of the substrate is the next step. The wood strips stiffen the surface, which is helpful when installing long countertops. The wood also gives the vulnerable front edge of the countertop some extra hardness and durability, and it accepts contact cement better than the porous cut edges of the particleboard.

**MAKE JOINTS STRONG, STRAIGHT, AND SMOOTH.**
If you can't avoid a joint, try to plan the least-obtrusive place to join the particleboard pieces that will make up the countertop. Overlapping two pieces allows you to mark the exact location of the joint. You can cut particleboard to size with a circular saw. For smooth, straight edges, run the saw against a straightedge guide.

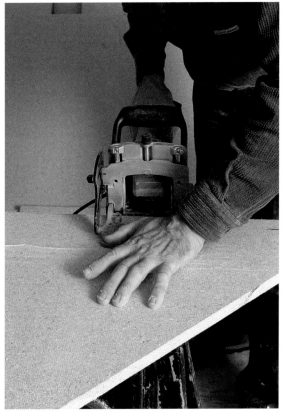

## Be Careful with the Laminate

Until it is glued to the substrate, plastic laminate tears and cracks easily. It is important to treat large pieces carefully. I leave the laminate rolled up in the box until I am ready to work with it. Laminate can be cut in various ways, but I use a laminate trimmer or a small router with a sharp laminate bit. A dull bit will chip the laminate.

The laminate is first cut oversize, then trimmed after it is glued to the substrate. I clamp the sheet of laminate to a large table or a sheet of plywood and cut 3-in.-wide strips for the edges. Then I cut the top pieces of laminate on the prepared substrate, where I can follow the shape of the countertop. The cutoffs must be supported or they will crack.

Joining pieces of laminate is tricky. Never rely on the factory edge of the laminate to be straight. If you are joining large sheets, use a laminate trimmer or a router with a straightedge and trim both pieces to make sure they are straight and square.

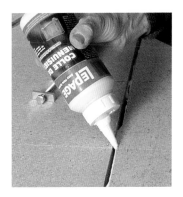 

**BISCUITS AND BOLTS WORK TOGETHER.** Mark biscuit locations every 6 in. A pencil line across the joint is all you need to align the biscuit joiner. Bond each joint with yellow glue. Hidden on the underside of the substrate, countertop bolts clamp the joint together.

Cut edge strips to length with a miter saw. Sandwich the laminate strip between two scraps of particleboard, and make the cut through the particleboard and the laminate.

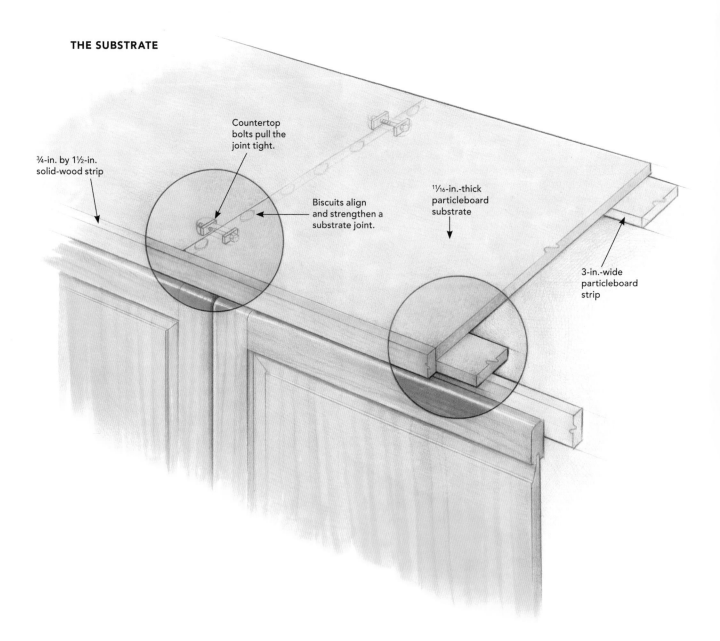

¾-in. by 1½-in.
solid-wood strip

Countertop
bolts pull the
joint tight.

Biscuits align
and strengthen a
substrate joint.

1¹/₁₆-in.-thick
particleboard
substrate

3-in.-wide
particleboard
strip

## Laminate the Edges First

Contact cement is sticky, so work slowly when you
are gluing the laminate. Once you glue down a piece
of laminate, you probably won't be able to get it off.

I use latex contact cement because it is nontoxic
and nonflammable (www.lepageproducts.com). Both
the laminate and the substrate get two thin coats of
contact cement. Two thin coats dry faster than one
thick coat. Because the particleboard will absorb
some of the contact cement, the first coat is used
to seal the pores, whereas the second coat remains
on the surface, where I want it. Allow the contact

cement to dry completely between coats and before
applying the laminate to the particleboard.

The edges are laminated and trimmed first. After
the edge strips all are applied, I press them to the
substrate with a roller. I use a heat gun to bend edge
strips into and around radiused corners. Heating the
laminate helps to prevent cracking as it bends. Pushing a heated edge piece into a curved inside corner
is more difficult than turning an outside corner.
Any voids that are left between the laminate and
the substrate will be filled with epoxy before the top
laminate goes on.

**DOUBLE UP THE PERIMETER.** Build up the edges with particleboard strips. On the edges that will be laminated, attach the strips flush with the top. On the back edges, recess the strips about ¼ in. to ease any scribing that has to be done. Glue and nail solid-wood strips along the front edge. The wood strips stiffen longer surfaces and accept contact cement better than the cut edge of particleboard.

To trim the edge pieces flush, I usually use a bearing-guided flush-trimming bit, which can be chucked in a laminate trimmer or a small router. After the edges are trimmed, I give the top of the substrate a final check to make sure it's flat and smooth. Slight irregularities near the front edge—between the particleboard, the wood edging, and the laminate—can be removed with a file or a belt sander.

## Align the Top Sheet Carefully

Before contact cement is applied to the top of the substrate or the large sheets of laminate, these surfaces should be dusted thoroughly with a brush or air hose to remove debris. Even a tiny piece of debris will show through the laminate.

To line up large sheets of laminate without letting them touch the glued-up substrate, I use Venetian-blind slats as spacers. The laminate is placed on top of the spacers and positioned as it will lay on the substrate. Starting in the middle of the countertop, I work my way toward the ends, removing the spacers and pressing down the laminate. To ensure a good bond, I use a roller to press the laminate to the substrate.

If I find an air bubble, I heat the laminate from the bubble to the nearest edge to create an exit for the air. If that doesn't work, I can drill a small hole (¹⁄₁₆ in.) through the bottom of the substrate to get the air out from under the laminate.

The oversize sheet of laminate then can be trimmed around the edges of the countertop. Use a light touch with the laminate trimmer or router to avoid marking or scratching the laminated edges. Because the cut edges of the laminate can be sharp, the last thing I do is lightly file the top and bottom edges and all the corners with a hand file.

**EDGES FIRST.** After adhering a laminate edge strip along the front edge of the countertop, trim it flush. A bearing-guided flush-trimming bit gets the job done.

**LATEX DOESN'T STINK.** Use a roller to apply two coats of latex contact cement to the substrate and the laminate. Make sure the contact cement is dry on both surfaces before gluing them together. Spacers keep the two adhesive-coated surfaces apart while you position the large top sheet of laminate. When you're ready, remove the spacers, starting in the middle of the countertop and working out toward the edges.

# THREE TIPS FOR WORKING WITH LAMINATE

**1** Use Venetian-blind slats as spacers between the substrate and laminate sheets to make sure the laminate is aligned properly before the two glued-up surfaces are allowed to touch.

**2** For a clean-cut laminate edge, first cut a longer strip than you need. Then put the end of the strip between two scraps of particleboard and cut it with a miter saw.

**3** Laminate warmed up with a heat gun or a hair dryer is easy to bend. Pull the laminate gently while applying heat. At first the laminate will resist, but after a few minutes, it will bend.

**1** Venetian blinds make great spacers.

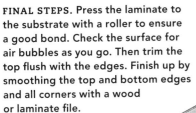

**FINAL STEPS.** Press the laminate to the substrate with a roller to ensure a good bond. Check the surface for air bubbles as you go. Then trim the top flush with the edges. Finish up by smoothing the top and bottom edges and all corners with a wood or laminate file.

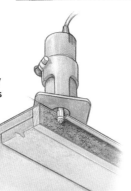

### SOURCES

**WILSONART**
www.wilsonart.com
800-433-3222

**FORMICA®**
www.formica.com
800-367-6422

2 A laminate sandwich makes for clean cuts.

3 Heat laminate to make it flexible.

# Making Wood Countertops

BY DAN VOS

The most common thing I hear when people first see my wood countertops is, "Wow, that's beautiful. But are wood countertops durable enough for a kitchen?" My answer is, "Mine are."

Having made a career of building wood countertops, I've developed construction methods and finishing techniques that make them both durable and beautiful. Beauty comes from the nature of wood itself, from the way I orient its grain, and from the finish I apply to it. Durability comes from design and construction specifications appropriate for the use of the top. For instance, no matter how much you love the way that it looks, a face-grain pine top is not an appropriate chopping surface. Pine is soft, and face-grain construction is not durable enough to handle pressure from knives.

My shop is production oriented, with special tools and work surfaces that allow us to build large, complicated countertops efficiently. But as you'll see in the process of making the face-grain walnut island counter shown here, all you need to make a wood counter is a large work surface, a jointer, a planer, a router, a random-orbit sander, and a handful of bar clamps. Before you jump into a countertop project, though, it's a good idea to explore the aesthetics and durability of different wood species and three types of construction for wood counters. Then you can determine if a top like this one is right for you.

## Expect Wood to Change Color and Move

I try to guide my clients toward a wood species and grain orientation that appeals to their aesthetics and also suits how they will use the countertop. Where nothing more than a tough chopping surface is what the client wants, I usually recommend an end-grain top of hard sugar maple (more on grain orientation later). When a homeowner wants visual interest, there are lots of wood species that make great face-grain or edge-grain tops. Among domestic hardwoods, cherry, walnut, beech, and oak are good choices; among tropical hardwoods, sipo, santos, African mahogany, and jatoba (Brazilian cherry) are all stable and are all easy to work with.

I don't get caught up with the hardness ratings of various wood species, but I avoid some that are either inordinately difficult to work or are better suited to outdoor use, such as cypress, cedar, and hemlock. Also, some of the superhard tropical woods, such as bloodwood and ipé, have problems with end-checking.

Bear in mind that wood can change color over time due to age, ambient conditions, or the type of finish you use. For example, the tung oil–based finishes I use bring out amber tones in lighter woods, and they deepen and enrich darker species.

**FACE GRAIN.** With the milled faces of each board oriented up, face-grain tops are typically the easiest to glue up. They are not the most durable or knife-friendly counters, but if wood grain and color are what you're after, this type of construction may be right for you. See this walnut top built on the following pages.

**END GRAIN.** End-grain, or butcher-block, counters like this teak top are the most functional. Not only can they handle repeated chopping but they're also self-healing. Maintenance is as simple as occasional applications of mineral oil. These busy-looking tops are the most challenging to build.

**EDGE GRAIN.** Ripping flatsawn stock into strips and gluing them up on edge creates a top that has less of the color and grain characteristics of a face-grain top but more durability. As seen in this mesquite island top, it takes a lot of 1-in. to 2-in. strips to make an edge-grain top, so the glue-up is a bit more challenging.

MILL THE STOCK. For a standard 1½-in.-thick countertop, I start with 2-in. roughsawn boards. I buy boards longer than I need and have enough material to make the blank wider than the finished top will be. Before choosing or arranging boards, I skip-plane each one (see the top board in the photo at left) to reveal its grain, color, and blemishes.

PREPARE THE SURFACES' MATING EDGES. Use a jointer or a router and guide to create one perfectly straight edge. If you use the latter technique, rip the board on a tablesaw, removing just enough material to create a parallel straightedge. Flatten the board on a jointer and plane it to within ⅛₂ in. of final thickness. The remaining ⅛₂ in. will be removed later when the blank is sanded.

Once you determine which species to use, make sure to buy kiln-dried stock to minimize the potential for movement. I test one or two boards from every order to be sure the moisture content is between 6 percent and 9 percent. Still, every board and every top will move, especially across the grain. You have to take that movement into account when you build and install a wood top.

To balance the stresses between boards, it is a good practice to alternate the growth-ring pattern in the glue-up. It is also a good idea to turn boards frequently during the planing and jointing process.

Working both sides of the boards before glue-up can remove some of their internal stresses and reduce their propensity to go their own way. If you have time, you also should acclimate the wood to the site before gluing up the counter.

To accommodate wood movement when installing wood counters, I fasten them through slotted screw holes. For tops held tight to a wall, you can use a matching backsplash to hide seasonal gaps or slot only the screw holes nearest the overhanging areas. The top should transfer most of its stress toward the path of least resistance.

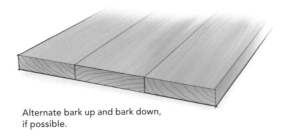

Alternate bark up and bark down, if possible.

**LAY OUT FOR LOOKS FIRST.** Pick the best face of each board, and lay the boards side by side. To help keep the top flat over time, try to arrange them so that they alternate bark up and bark down (see the drawing at right). But don't sacrifice a perfect face for a top that will be well fastened to the cabinets. Draw a triangle across all the boards to maintain the arrangement.

**TIP**

IF THE BOARDS JOIN NICELY at the center but the ends are open, you need to get the edges straighter. If the opposite is true and you're making a long top, you can rely on clamps to close a gap up to 1⁄16 in. Springing the joint in this manner builds stress into the top that actually counters potential wood movement.

## Build It for the Way You'll Use It

When homeowners say they want a "pretty" wood counter, I usually end up building a face-grain top like the one featured here. The wide face of a board is where color and grain come alive. However, the cost of the rift-sawn, quartersawn, and flitchsawn stock that I commonly choose for these tops can be significantly more than what you would pay for suitable edge- or end-grain materials. Face-grain tops have pros and cons when it comes to durability. A teak face-grain top, for example, is an excellent choice for sink areas because it likes water, but you'll cry wet tears on it the first time it's marked by a knife.

When I'm putting together a face-grain top, much more effort goes into the pre-glue-up layout than with other kinds of tops. I skip-plane both faces of the rough boards to reveal flaws, color, and grain before choosing which to use. Then I carefully lay out the boards, keeping visual characteristics and internal-stress characteristics in mind until I'm satisfied with the balance of cosmetics and stability. Just before finishing, I spend extra time with face-grain tops, detailing small flaws with colored epoxy. Gluing up a face-grain top, however, is easier than gluing up edge- or end-grain counters because there are typically fewer boards to join.

Edge-grain tops offer the best combination of durability, beauty, and cost. When made from boards 1 in. to 2 in. wide, they can show a lot of color and a straight, elegant grain pattern, but when used for food prep and chopping, edge-grain tops scar and acquire a patina. The glue-up is more involved with edge-grain tops than with face-grain tops because there are more glue joints. Here, you can save money on lumber by starting with flatsawn boards that will be ripped and can be oriented to reveal a rift-sawn or quartersawn face.

**GLUE UP THE BLANK.** For most tops, I use Titebond II® (or Titebond II Extend for a few more minutes of open time). On oily tropical hardwoods, I use West System® epoxy (105 resin and 205 hardener). Glue joints are generally stronger than wood, so I don't biscuit the tops for strength. Sometimes I use them for alignment. For tops wider than 36 in. or that use more than five boards, consider gluing up the top in two halves and then gluing the halves together. Leave the top clamped for at least four hours, preferably overnight.

**GLUE BOTH FACES LIBERALLY.** Starting about 3 in. in from the ends, space clamps every 12 in. Top clamps will be placed between the bottom clamps after the glue is applied. Start with an outside board, tip it up, and run a glue-line down the middle. You can't put on too much glue, but you can use too little. Use a solder brush to spread glue.

**ADD PRESSURE A LITTLE AT A TIME.** Start by tightening the middle clamp just enough to hold the top together. Check the joints for alignment, and tighten the remaining clamps from the outside, bottom clamp first, then top, then bottom, and so on. Check the top with a straightedge between clamps. Cupping reveals uneven pressure. You'll need to loosen the clamps and start again. Scrape away glue squeeze-out with a putty knife.

End-grain counters are the last word in chopping. They are resistant to scarring, are self-healing, are easy on fine knife edges, and soak up finishes like nobody's business. But end grain is a busy look. There are lots of glue joints and lots of growth rings. Performance comes at a price, too. Not only are these the most expensive tops I make, but because of the laborious construction process, they're also the most difficult to manage in the shop, being fussy to put together and somewhat brittle until installed. It doesn't matter what type of stock you use for an end-grain top as long as it is all the same. In this way, the individual pieces expand and contract similarly.

## Be Prepared to Work Quickly

I'm often asked what tools are absolutely essential, even for someone planning to build only one wood countertop. I think that a 10-in. tablesaw, a 6-in. jointer, and a portable planer are important to get the job done right. I assume that anyone planning to build a countertop has a router and a random-orbit sander. The number of bar clamps you need depends on the length of the top, but a general rule is one clamp per foot, plus one.

I started making wood tops as an amateur woodworker, and the biggest mistake I made back then was not sufficiently planning for handling and working large boards and slabs. Today, I've tweaked my production shop to the nth degree. I have plenty of handling clearance, but I keep machines close enough to make it easy to move materials around. You might not have the luxury of a space as large as mine, but with careful planning before you begin to build, you can spare yourself a lot of unnecessary frustration.

The first steps require milling long boards with a planer and jointer and ripping them on a tablesaw or with a circular saw and straightedge. Here, dust control is an important consideration. For the remainder of the work, you need a well-lit open space, preferably a workbench, though you can glue up a top on the floor. The space should be easy to keep clean, within reach of an outlet, and easy to maneuver around from all sides.

**MAKE SHAPES AND CUTOUTS WITH A TEMPLATE.** First, use the template to trace the shape on the top. Rough-cut the shape with a jigsaw; then use the template again to guide a router and pattern bit to shape the top. Use the same process for sink cutouts, but work with the top upside down. This way, you can screw the template to the top.

**FILL KNOTS AND BLEMISHES WITH EPOXY.** After scraping away any loose material, use five-minute epoxy with a coloring dye (www.homesteadfinishingproducts.com) to fill knots and other blemishes.

**SAND, THEN SAND MORE.** With 60-grit sandpaper on a random-orbit sander, correct any cosmetic defects, paying special attention to the joints. Use a straight-edge to make sure that the top is perfectly flat. Sand with 80-, 100-, 120-, and 180-grit sandpaper. Start sanding the edges once you've gotten to the 120-grit paper. Wet the top with mineral spirits to reveal remaining defects.

**PROFILE THE EDGES.** Use a bottom-mount, bearing-guided router bit. Depending on the profile, you might need to make multiple passes. Sand the profile with 120- to 180-grit sandpaper. Soften or ease all sharp edges. Finally, sand the entire top to 220-grit.

**CUT TO LENGTH AND WIDTH, PARALLEL AND SQUARE.** I make the blank approximately 2 in. longer and ¾ in. wider than needed so that the first step out of the clamps is to cut it to size. With a circular saw outfitted with a high-quality blade and edge guide, rip one of the long edges. Measure across for a parallel rip. Repeat this process to crosscut the ends if they're being cut square.

Once you begin the glue-up, you have to work quickly. You have only about eight minutes, so take the time to get the clamps spaced out and ready to use and have glue bottles, brushes, and cleanup supplies close at hand. It's also a good idea to have someone available to help because a lot needs to happen during those eight minutes.

When the clamps come off, you'll have to manage the large, heavy blank. Consider making a simple cart with heavy-duty casters. You also should make screw blocks (¾-in. plywood cut into 2-in. by 3-in. pieces, with a 1⅝-in. drywall screw flush-set through one side). The screw blocks are used to raise the top above the work surface to allow air to circulate, which helps prevent the top from warping and cupping, and to make it easier to apply finish to the edges.

# INSTALL IT WITH MOVEMENT IN MIND

### USE SLOTTED SCREW HOLES
Fastening the counter through elongated screw holes in the bracing at the top of the cabinet allows the counter to move freely as the boards expand and contract.

### DON'T USE ADHESIVES UNLESS YOU HAVE TO
If you glue down the top, it won't be able to move and can crack. Bar tops set on pony walls or other narrow edges, however, may need adhesive to keep the top stable.

### SUPPORT OVERHANGS
An overhang more than 4 in. on an edge should have support such as a corbel or a decorative or hidden bracket. Overhanging ends, on the other hand, need no extra support. In this direction, the wood countertop is inherently strong.

### SITE MODIFICATIONS NEED TO BE SEALED
If you scribe the countertop to fit tightly to a wall or cabinet or make a penetration for a faucet or sink on site, be sure to reapply finish to the cut area.

### KEEP WATER FROM GETTING TRAPPED
Standing water will eventually erode even the most durable materials. No matter what type of sink or faucet you install, make sure to apply a heavy bead of caulk between the sink or faucet and countertop.

## Renewable Finishes for a Long-Lasting Countertop

Like choosing a wood species and construction technique, I choose the most appropriate finish based on how the top will be used. For tough, hard, built-up protection, I use Waterlox®, which combines the amber tone of tung oil with hardeners to create a film on the surface of the counter. For tops that will be used for food preparation, I use a mix of tung oil and citrus solvent, which is food safe. This penetrating finish cures in the grain but doesn't build up on the surface. For smaller end-grain chopping blocks, regular applications of mineral oil are sufficient. These finishes are easy to repair and renew, which is the key to a long-lasting wood countertop, and both are water resistant.

Whichever finish I'm using, I work in a finishing room isolated from the dust and debris of the fabrication shop. If you don't have this luxury, make sure to clean the work area before finishing. And even though these finishes are safe, make sure you have adequate ventilation and wear gloves.

**FINISH THE COUNTER.** For most tops, I use one of two tung oil–based finishes: Waterlox or a 50/50 mix of pure tung oil and citrus solvent, shown here. No matter what finish I'm using, I coat all surfaces, including the bottom. While I work, the top rests on the tips of drywall screws driven through small plywood blocks placed atop the worktable.

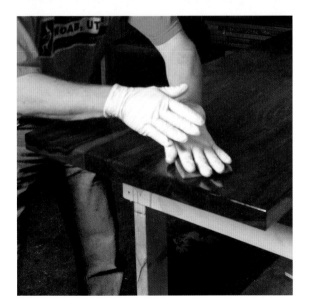

**FLOOD AND WIPE THE FIRST COATS.** A wood counter lets you know how much finish it needs by the way it absorbs (or doesn't). Most wood species suck up the first two coats, so start by flooding the top with a foam brush. After a few minutes, wipe off the excess finish.

**WET-SAND THE LAST COAT.** When the counter stops absorbing the finish at a dramatic rate, likely by the third coat, apply the finish, and wet-sand it with fine foam sanding pads. Once you've sanded the entire top, wipe off the excess finish. Use a power buffer to bring the finished top to life.

# A New Approach to Concrete Countertops

BY BUDDY RHODES

Concrete countertops have become popular over the past 20 years, and with good reason. Of course, they look great. Because they're cast, they can be made in almost any shape or style, and unlike other counter materials they're practically bombproof. Best of all, almost anyone can make one with a few basic tools, which brings the price below that of most other materials.

I began working with concrete about 30 years ago. I made countertops, benches, big planters, and decorative tiles. Most of these were made either with a traditional aggregate mix or a dry-pack technique I devised that yields a variegated look. Made in molds, the objects were finished by hand-troweling or by rubbing with successively finer abrasive pads.

A few years ago I started fooling with a technique borrowed from the world of commercial concrete. For some time now, fabricators have made exterior panels for high-rise buildings with a mix that yields a strong, lightweight concrete. Their secret is to substitute fiberglass fibers and mesh for the traditional steel reinforcement. Because there's no need to bed the steel reinforcement in inches of concrete, the concrete can be made as thin as $1\frac{1}{4}$ in. Perhaps best of all, the finished surface is sprayed into the form before the rest of the concrete is added, which cancels the need for almost all the surface polishing and work at the end of the project.

Here, I'll show how I made a vanity counter and integral sink bound for *Fine Homebuilding*'s Project House. (I'd like to give credit to Brandon Gore for his inspiration and for teaching me how to fabric form a sink.) The first step in the process is to make the mold for the sink from fiberglass-resin-impregnated cloth and plywood, then attach it to the countertop form. Once it's complete, I use a drywall-texture spray gun to coat the form with a thin layer of tinted concrete, then mix a thicker batch with fiberglass fibers and hand-pack it to the final thickness. When the concrete has cured, the counter is nearly complete and needs only a light buffing and a couple of coats of sealer before being installed.

## Start with the Sink Mold

The first step in making the mold is to determine the shape of the sink. You can make a sink in almost any shape or depth, as long as it directs water to the drain. The depth of the bowl is established by plywood ribs glued to a base that represents the sink rim. This frame then is covered with resin-impregnated cloth that hardens into a negative of the sink bowl. The trick here is to use different forms of

MOLD THE SINK. The first step is to build the sink mold, which represents the inside, rather than the outside, of the sink. It starts as a plywood structure that's then tightly wrapped with polyester cloth, coated with fiberglass and polyester resins, and sanded smooth. The sink mold begins with a base of ¾-in. melamine that's cut to the shape of the bowl's lip. Temporary backer ribs pocket-screwed to the back provide rigidity. The depth of the bowl is defined by ⅜-in. bending plywood hot-glued to the base. A length of pipe sets the location and depth of the drain.

NO WRINKLES. The foundation for the mold is a piece of polyester-fleece material (available from a fabric supply store) that's stretched tightly over the form and stapled to the edge of the base.

POLYESTER ON POLYESTER. The first base coat is a two-part fiberglass resin (3M®) that's applied with a brush over the form so that the material is coated. Be sure to wear an organic-vapor respirator when applying the resin. Set it aside to dry overnight.

BUILD A SMOOTH COAT. After sanding the base coat, mix auto-body filler (Bondo®) into a batch of the same fiberglass resin until it has the consistency of thick molasses. Pour it onto the form, and use a brush to coat the form evenly. Let it dry, then sand smooth.

**CREATE THE COUNTER FORM.** The counter form needs to be flat and smooth. The easiest way to make a form is to lay out the shape on a full sheet of ¾-in. melamine. Strips of melamine screwed to the sheet define the edges and depth of the counter. (The depth in this instance was 1½ in.) If needed, make the form for the backsplash at the same time.

polyester—polyester fleece cloth, two-part fiberglass resin, and auto-body filler—that bond together perfectly.

Here, I wanted a fairly conventional bowl, so I started with the shape of the rim, which was an oval with squared-off ends. After cutting out the shape from a piece of melamine, I attached 4-in.-wide reinforcing ribs to the form base with pocket screws. These ribs keep the shape from deforming during the resin's curing process.

After I determine the depth and profile of the bowl, I cut out four pieces of ⅜-in. bending plywood, one for each side of the bowl. I attach them to the base with small blocks and hot glue. I cover this structure with polyester cloth (otherwise known as fleece, the same stuff they make pajamas from).

After coating the sink form, then sanding and sealing it, I lay out the shape of the counter with 1½-in.-wide strips of melamine (the final thickness of the counter) screwed down on edge on a full sheet of ¾-in. melamine. While I'm at it, I make on the same sheet a form for a 4-in.-wide backsplash that's ¾ in. thick.

Remember that any imperfection in the form will be passed on to the counter, so everything should be as smooth as possible. Once I've placed the sink mold, I detail the form by filling all corners with silicone caulk and screw holes with modeling clay. Knockouts displace the areas meant for plumbing, such as the faucets and drain. Because wood absorbs water from the concrete and swells, it can't be removed once the counter has dried, so knockouts should be made from Styrofoam® or cast rubber. I make mine with VytaFlex® 40, a two-part urethane rubber from Smooth-On®.

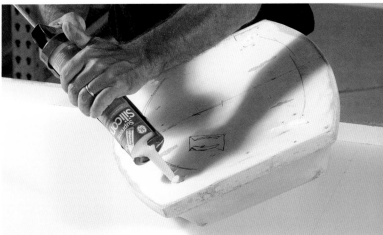

**ATTACH THE SINK MOLD.** After trimming away any excess along the sink mold's bottom edge, mark the sink location on the counter form. Squeeze a bead of silicone caulk onto the sink bottom and press it firmly into position.

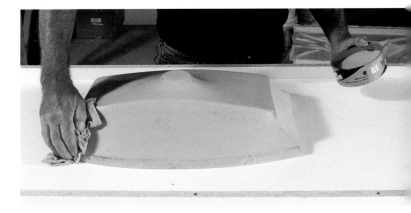

**WAX EARLY, WAX OFTEN.** There's no such thing as too much form release, so it's a good idea to apply three coats of butcher's wax to the completed form before spraying.

## SHOPMADE BEADING TOOL

I USE THIS TOOL TO CREATE a consistent profile in the freshly silicone-caulked joints, which form the slight radiused edge of the counter. I made it by gluing a ¼-in.-dia. ball bearing with epoxy onto the end of a 3-in.-long bolt.

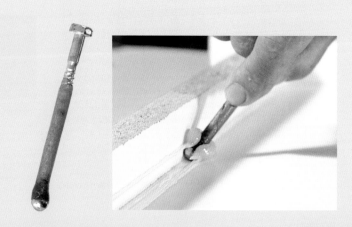

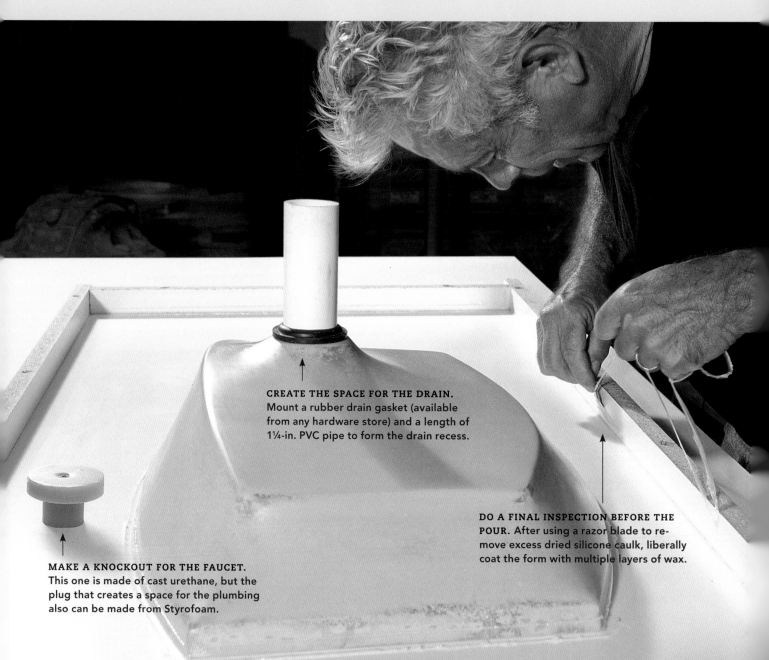

**CREATE THE SPACE FOR THE DRAIN.** Mount a rubber drain gasket (available from any hardware store) and a length of 1¼-in. PVC pipe to form the drain recess.

**MAKE A KNOCKOUT FOR THE FAUCET.** This one is made of cast urethane, but the plug that creates a space for the plumbing also can be made from Styrofoam.

**DO A FINAL INSPECTION BEFORE THE POUR.** After using a razor blade to remove excess dried silicone caulk, liberally coat the form with multiple layers of wax.

## A BIG SPRAY GUN

To get an even, smooth texture on the counter's surface, the first layers must be sprayed, and the easiest way to spray the mix is with a hopper-fed spray gun (see the photo at left), commonly known as a popcorn gun. It's typically used to apply plaster textures to ceilings, but it also will handle heavier mixtures. With a little practice, the gun is easy to use, but it requires an air compressor. I use a model called the SharpShooter®, which is made by Marshalltown®.

SPRAY IN THE COUNTER'S FINISH SURFACE. For this technique, the first layer of concrete in the form gives the sink its smooth surface. The mix is sprayed in two coats, each about ⅛ in. thick. For every 25 lb. of spray mix (portland-cement-to-sand ratio of 1:1), the mix uses 1½ qt. of water, ½ qt. of curing compound, 2 oz. of water reducer, and 220g of pigment. Mix in a 19-gal. bucket, liquids first, then add half the dry mix at a time.

THIN AND WET. Because this layer is sprayed, it must have a thin consistency. Mix the liquids first in a 19-gal. bucket with a paddle in a ½-in. drill, then add the dry ingredients in stages. Note the shop-vacuum hose, which helps to control the dust during the mix. A dust mask is required equipment.

## Spray the First Layers of Concrete

The finished surface of the counter is made by spraying a thin mix of portland cement and sand with a popcorn sprayer. The most important thing at this stage is to make sure that the spray coats are applied uniformly to the surface of the form. When spraying, try to keep a consistent distance between the gun and the form, and sweep the gun back and forth in a slow, fluid motion. If you're not familiar with the technique of spraying, it's a good idea to practice on a piece of cardboard first to get a feel for the process.

The layer that gives the counter its strength is a mixture of concrete, glass fibers, and mesh. The fiberglass has been treated so that it won't break down in the highly alkaline environment of the concrete.

I apply handfuls of the fairly dry mix to make a 1-in. layer. After packing around the drain plug, I use a trowel to level the area directly at the base of the plug. I also check that I haven't left any voids, especially around the knockouts.

MAKE SURE THE SPRAY IS EVENLY DISTRIBUTED. After the first coat, use a chip brush to push the wet mix into any voids that might create air pockets in the surface.

# FORM THE OVERFLOW DRAIN

To create the sink's overflow drain, first apply a 1½-in.-wide, ½-in.-thick strip of Styrofoam reinforced with packing tape on the side of the sink mold's outer edge so that it extends from the drain stub to about 1 in. from the sink rim. Cover the strip with the same depth of backing mix. After you remove the counter from the form, use a masonry bit to drill a ½-in. hole just below the sink rim where the end of the Styrofoam sits. Pour a few tablespoons of lacquer thinner through an empty caulk-tube funnel into the hole. The solvent dissolves the foam, leaving the open overflow drain.

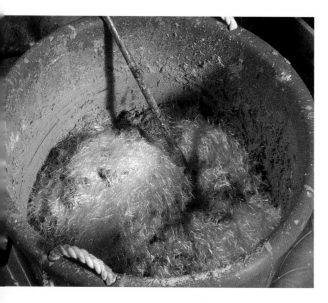

ADD CONCRETE, FIBER, AND MESH. This counter derives its strength from fiberglass fibers and mesh. Start the mix with 5 qt. of water, 2 qt. of curing compound, and 8 oz. of water reducer, then add 2 lb. of powdered dye and mix well. Next, add 100 lb. of the portland cement/sand mix (no aggregate), and when fully combined, fold in 2 lb. of alkaline-resistant fiberglass fibers. It's important not to break the fibers with excessive mixing.

ADD MESH FOR SUPPORT. Along the length of the counter, lay a piece of 4-in.-wide fiberglass mesh on each side of the sink, then cover it with the backing mix. The mesh should extend over the sink bowl.

After filling the form, I cover it with a plastic sheet, which keeps the concrete from curing too quickly, and leave it overnight. The next day, I remove the form sides and, with the help of an assistant, flip over the counter. We support it on two identically sized buckets, one on each side of the sink.

## Finish Touch-Ups

The best part about this method is that once the counter is out of the form, there's little finishing to do. To fill the pin holes left by air bubbles, I make a paste of portland cement, dye, and water and squeegee it into the surface. When it's dry, I lightly buff the counter with a nylon abrasive pad. Finally, I apply three coats of sealer: first, a penetrating sealer; second, a satin sealer; and third, a coat of beeswax. They are absorbed into the surface and protect it.

**PACK AND SMOOTH.** Apply the backing mix by packing handfuls onto the form. The backing should have a consistent thickness of about 1¼ in. everywhere in the form. Use a float to smooth the final surface.

# UNMOLDING THE COUNTER

**WITH THE AMOUNT OF MOLD RELEASE USED,** you'd think the counter would pop out in a hurry, but it rarely does. After driving two screws into the melamine sink-form top, we tried to lever it out, but the screws just pulled out. Compressed air didn't work either. Finally, I cut an oblong hole in the top and supported a short 2×4 with blocks on each side. We attached two short bar clamps to the 2×4 and underneath the hole, then tightened the clamps at the same rate until the mold popped out.

## CONTRIBUTORS

**Rex Alexander** is a kitchen designer and cabinetmaker in Fenton, Mich.

**Brent Benner** runs The Roxbury Cabinet Company (www.roxbury cabinet.com) in Roxbury, Conn.

**Andy Engel** is a senior *Fine Homebuilding* editor.

**Rick Gedney** owns Kitchens by Gedney (www.gedneykitchens .com) in Madison, Conn.

**Scott Gibson**, a contributing writer to *Fine Homebuilding*, lives in Southern Maine.

**Jamie Gold**, CKD, CAPS, is a Certified Kitchen Designer in San Diego and the author of *New Kitchen Ideas That Work* (Taunton Press, 2012). You can find her designs and blog online at www.jgkitchens.com.

**Mike Guertin**, the editorial adviser to *Fine Homebuilding*, is a builder and remodeler in East Greenwich, R.I.

**Philip Hansell** is a painter in Durham, N.C.

**Sven Hanson** is a cabinetmaker in Marietta, Ga., and Albuquerque, N.M.

**David Hart** is a full-time freelance writer and retired tile contractor from Rice, Virginia.

**Nancy R. Hiller** (www.nrhiller design.com) is a professional maker of custom furniture and cabinetry based in Bloomington, Ind. She specializes in period-authentic furniture and built-ins for homes and offices from the late-19th through mid-20th centuries.

**Ian Ingersoll** designs and builds furniture at his shop in West Cornwall, Conn.

**Joseph Lanza** (www.josephlanza .com) designs and builds entire houses, as well as their parts, in Duxbury, Mass.

**Nena Donovan Levine**, Allied ASID, NKBA, is a kitchen and bath designer in West Hartford, Conn.

**Mike Maines** (www.michael-maines.com) is a designer, builder and woodworker in Palermo, Maine.

**Tom Meehan** and his wife, Lane, are owners of Cape Cod Tileworks, a full-service tile store in Harwich, Mass.

**Isaak Mester** has been in the construction business for 28 years. Although he has tackled all phases of residential construction, he has concentrated on kitchens and baths during the last 10 years. In an acknowledgment of his sore shoulders and knees, Isaak has become a licensed building and plumbing inspector.

**Steve Morris** is a finish carpenter and kitchen installer in Sarnia, Ontario, Canada.

**Buddy Rhodes** has been at the leading edge of concrete design in both residential and commercial applications for the past 20 years. Lately, he's been working with a new lightweight concrete mix that doesn't need traditional reinforcement, so the material can be much thinner. His company Buddy Rhodes products (www.buddy rhodes.com) merged in 2012 with Delta Performance and Blue Concrete to provide the most up-to-date concrete products.

Jennifer Stimpson is a former editorial intern with *Fine Homebuilding*.

Gary Striegler, a frequent contributor to *Fine Homebuilding*, is a custom-home builder in Fayetteville, Ark. He teaches each summer at the Marc Adams school of Woodworking and works with Mercy International on building projects in Honduras.

Matthew Teague is a professional furniture maker and the editorial director of Spring House Press.

Dan Vos owns DeVos Custom Woodworking (www.devoswoodworking.com) in Dripping Springs, Texas.

Rob Yagid is design editor at *Fine Homebuilding*.

# CREDITS

All photos are courtesy of *Fine Homebuilding* magazine © The Taunton Press, Inc., except as noted below.

The articles in this book appeared in the following issues of *Fine Homebuilding*:

pp. 5–11: Refinish Your Cabinets by Philip Hansel, issue 240. Photos by Patrick McCombe.

pp. 12–19: A Buyer's Guide to Kitchen Cabinets by Scott Gibson, issue 191. Photos by Charles Miller except for the left and right photos p. 12 and the photos pp. 16-17 by Krysta S. Doerfler.

pp. 20–27: Souped-Up Stock Cabinets by Gary Striegler, issue 175. Photos by Roe A. Osborn. Drawings by Bob La Pointe.

pp. 28–37: Get to Know Semicustom Cabinets by Nena Donovan Levine, issue 242. Photos courtesy of the manufacturers.

pp. 38–41: Build Better Cabinets with the Best Plywood by Matthew Teague, issue 210. Photos by Rodney Diaz except for the photos p. 41 courtesy of Columbia Forest Products. Drawing by Bill Godfrey.

pp. 42–49: 6 Rules for Fast and Foolproof Cabinetmaking by Sven Hanson, issue 177. Photos by Daniel S. Morrison except for the photo p. 42 by Robert Reck.

pp. 50–57: A Faster, Easier Approach to Custom Cabinets by Mike Maines, issue 200. Photos by Rob Yagid. Drawing by Bob La Pointe.

pp. 58–65: A New Approach to Classic Cabinets by Mike Maines, issue 244. Photos by Brian McAward except for the photo p. 58 by Nat Rea.

pp. 66–68: Building Skills: Making an arched cabinet face-frame rail by Gary Striegler, issue 212. Photos by Charles Bickford except for the bottom right photo p. 68 by John Ross. Drawing by Dan Thornton.

pp. 69–72: Building Skills: Making raised-panel doors on a tablesaw by Rex Alexander, issue 177. Photos by Roe A. Osborn except for the right photo p. 70 by Bill Duckworth. Drawing by Dan Thornton.

pp. 73–76: Master Carpenter: Beaded cabinet openings by Gary Striegler, issue 170. Photos by Roe A. Osborn. Drawings by Vince Babak.

pp. 77–79: Master Carpenter: Dress up cabinet face frames with a mitered integral bead by Brent Benner, issue 200. Photos by Charles Bickford except for the bottom left photo p. 78 by Krysta S. Doerfler. Drawings by Dan Thornton.

pp. 80–89: Installing Semicustom Cabinets by Isaak Mester, issue 241. Photos by Charles Bickford except for the photo p. 82 by John Ross.

pp. 90–99: Installing Kitchen Cabinets Smooth and Solo by Mike Guertin, issue 174. Photos by Brian Pontolilo except for the photo p. 90 by Nat Rea and the bottom left photo p. 94 courtesy of E-Z Spread N' Lift Industries.

pp. 100–107: How to Install Inset Cabinet Doors by Scott Gibson, issue 226. Photos by Charles Bickford except for the photo p. 100 and the bottom photo p. 105 by Nat Rea.

pp. 108–115: Crown Molding for Kitchen Cabinets by Gary Striegler, issue 244. Photos by Andy Engel except for the photo p. 109 by Bryan Striegler. Drawings by Bob La Pointe.

pp. 117–123: Build a Floating Vanity by Nancy Hiller, issue 236. Photos by Charles Bickford except for the product photos pp. 120-121 by Rodney Diaz. Drawing by Bob La Pointe.

pp. 124–125: Yard-Sale Bureau Becomes a Bathroom Vanity by Mike Guertin, issue 182. Photos by Roe A. Osborn except for the top photo p. 125 by Mike Guertin and the bottom photo p. 125 by Krysta S. Doerfler. Drawing by Bob La Pointe.

pp. 126–133: Break Out of the Bathroom Vanity by Ian Ingersoll, issue 132. Photos by Mac Vassallo except for the top photo p. 133 by Jefferson Kolle. Drawings by Bob La Pointe.

pp. 134–137: A Clever Island with Drawers by Joseph Lanza, issue 239. Photos by Charles Bickford. Drawings by John Hartman.

pp. 138–145: Build a Kitchen Island by Rick Gedney, issue 232. Photos by Patrick McCombe except for the photo p. 138 and the top right photo p. 141 by Charles Bickford.

pp. 146–153: A Clever Kitchen Built-In by Nancy R. Hiller, issue 193. Photos by Kendall Reeves. Drawings by Bob La Pointe.

pp. 155–161: A Designers Guide to Countertops by Jamie Gold, issue 239. Photos by Rodney Diaz except for the photo p. 156 courtesy of Jamie Gold and the photos pp. 160–161 by Greg Riegler. The kitchen on p. 156 was designed by Jamie Gold Kitchen and Bath Design, LLC with

Terry Smith Cabinetry and Design and Kevin Heinly, AIA, all in San Diego. The kitchen on pp. 160–161 was designed by Cheryl Kees Clendenon of In Detail Interiors, Pensacola, FL.

pp. 162–173: Amazing Countertops by Rob Yagid, issue 194. Photos by Krysta S. Doerfler except for the center photo p. 163 courtesy of Totally Bamboo, the top photo p. 164 courtesy of Klip Biotechnologies LLC., the left photo p. 165 courtesy of ThinkGlass, the top photo p. 167 courtesy of Vetrazzo, the top left photo p. 169 courtesy of Alkemi, and the center photo p. 169 courtesy of Eleek Inc.

pp. 170–171: What's the difference: Metal Countertops by Nena Donovan Levine, issue 199. Photos by Dan Thornton except for the photo p. 170 by Charles Miller.

pp. 172–173: What's the difference: Stone Countertops by Jennifer Stimpson, issue 191. Photo by Krysta S. Doerfler.

pp. 174–177: Building Skills: Cut a laminate countertop for a sink by Andy Engel, issue 242. Product photos by Dan Thornton. All other photos by Patrick McCombe.

pp. 177–181: Tiling Over a Laminate Counter by David Hart, issue 130. Photos by Charles Bickford.

pp. 182–187: Tiling a Backsplash by Tom Meehan, issue 167. Photos by Lindsay Meehan.

pp. 188–195: Make Your Own Laminate Countertops by Steve Morris, issue 166. Photos by Brian Pontolilo except for the bottom photo p. 189 and the bit photo p. 194 by Scott Phillips and the three right photos p. 189 courtesy of Wilsonart. Drawings by Bob La Pointe.

pp. 196–203: Making Wood Countertops by Dan Vos, issue 209. Photos by Brian Pontolilo except for the bottom photo p. 197 by Dan Vos. Drawing by Dan Thornton.

pp. 204–211: A New Approach to Concrete by Buddy Rhodes, issue 234. Photos by Charles Bickford.

# INDEX

**R**

Radius, plotting, 67
Refinishing cabinets, 5–11
    about: overview of, 5
    gear for, 8
    preparing for, 6–8
    reassembly, 10–11
    spraying guidelines, 6, 8–10
    surface prep, 7–8
Rollouts, 17

**S**

Sanding
    finished edges before assembly, 45
    refinishing cabinets and, 7–8
Scrap-metal countertops, 168–69
Screws
    concealing, 88, 89, 94, 95
    for joining stiles, 95
    for mounting cabinets, 63, 95
Scribing, 63, 88–89, 123, 152, 190, 202
Semicustom cabinets. *See* Cabinets,
        semicustom
Shelves
    beaded openings and, 74
    drilling pin holes, 46–47, 55, 60
Sinks
    concrete countertop and, 205–11
    cutting laminate for, 174–76
    cutting openings for, 144
    islands with, 135, 139, 144
    tiling around, 177–78
    vanities with, 117–23, 124–25, 127–33
    wood countertops with, 202
Slate countertops, 173
Slides. *See* Drawer slides
Slot joinery, 62, 64
Soapstone countertops, 157, 173
Sources
    cabinet manufacturers, 19
    concrete, 166
    countertop materials, 158, 159, 163, 164,
        165, 166, 167, 168, 169, 195
    molding suppliers, 25
    semicustom cabinets, 35
Spraying finishes, 6, 8–10, 63
Squaring joints, 45
Stainless-steel countertops, 170
Stock cabinets. *See* Cabinets, stock
Storage units, specialty, 14, 18, 19, 31,
        146–53
Studs, finding/marking, 86, 87, 92

**T**

Tiling
    backerboard for, 177–78, 179–80
    backsplash, 182–87
    grouting, 181, 185–87
    installing, 181, 184–85
    laying out, 180–81, 182–84
    over laminate countertop, 177–81
    sealing, 185
    working around outlets, 186
Trammel points, 67

**V**

Vanity, bureau as, 124–25
Vanity, floating, 117–23
    about: overview of design, 117–18
    custom-veneer fronts, 121–22
    drawings, 118–19
    fasteners, 119
    finishing for wet areas, 122
    frame structure, 118–19
    installing on wall, 122–23
    strength of, 118–19
    strong box structure, 118–19, 120
Vanity, Shaker cabinet as, 127–33
    about: overview of, 127–29
    accommodating plumbing, 127
    constructing, 127–33
    dimensions, 127
    drawings, 130–31
    solid-surface top, 129, 133
Veneer
    benefits of, 16–17
    custom, 121–22
    doors with, 34, 121–22
    drawers with, 121–22
    finishing for wet areas, 122, 125
    grading, 41
    grain continuity, 118
    plywood, 38, 39, 41, 59–61
    rotary-cut, 41
    sliced, 41
    substrates for, 33

**W**

Wood
    cabinets. *See Cabinet and Vanity*
        *references*; Islands; Kitchen, built-
        in unit
    countertops. *See* Countertops, wood
    door types, 16–17
    poor quality, finish for, 133
    solid, joint considerations, 150–52

**Y**

Yard-sale bureau, as vanity, 124–25

**Z**

Zinc countertops, 170, 171

# If you like this book, you'll love *Fine Homebuilding*.